CLEP

College Level Examination Program

Sociology
Series

To obtain permission(s) to use the material from this work for any purpose including workshops or seminars, please submit a written request to:

XAMonline, Inc.
21 Orient Avenue
Melrose, MA 02176
Toll Free: 1-800-301-4647
Email: info@xamonline.com
Web: www.xamonline.com
Fax: 1-617-583-5552

Library of Congress Cataloging-in-Publication Data
Wynne, Sharon

CLEP Sociology Series/ Sharon Wynne
    ISBN: 978-1-60787-579-6

1. CLEP   2. Study Guides   3. Sociology

Disclaimer:
The opinions expressed in this publication are the sole works of XAMonline and were created independently from the College Board, or other testing affiliates. Between the time of publication and printing, specific test standards as well as testing formats and website information may change that are not included in part or in whole within this product. XAMonline develops sample test questions, and they reflect similar content as on real tests; however, they are not former tests. XAMonline assembles content that aligns with test standards but makes no claims nor guarantees candidates a passing score.

Cover photos by © Can Stock Photo Inc./GeorgiosArt/10056954; © Can Stock Photo Inc./ingridat/24290240; © Can Stock Photo Inc./scanrail/3495380; © Can Stock Photo Inc./kentoh/6613671; © Can Stock Photo Inc./lucidwaters/9437211

Printed in the United States of America
CLEP Sociology Series
ISBN: 978-1-60787-579-6

TABLE OF CONTENTS

Description of the Examination

The Human Growth and Development examination (Infancy, Childhood, Adolescence, Adulthood, and Aging) covers material that is generally taught in a one-semester introductory course in developmental psychology or human development. An understanding of the major theories and research related to the broad categories of physical development, cognitive development, and social development is required, as is the ability to apply this knowledge.

The examination contains approximately 90 questions to be answered in 90 minutes. Some of them are pretest questions that will not be scored. Any time candidates spend on tutorials and providing personal information is in addition to the actual testing time.

Knowledge and Skills Required

Questions on the Human Growth and Development examination require candidates to demonstrate one or more of the following abilities.

- Knowledge of basic facts and terminology
- Understanding of generally accepted concepts and principles
- Understanding of theories and recurrent developmental issues
- Applications of knowledge to particular problems or situations

The subject matter of the Human Growth and Development examination is drawn from the following categories. For each category, several key words and phrases identify topics with which candidates should be familiar. The percentages next to the main categories indicate the approximate percentage of exam questions on that topic.

10% Theoretical Perspectives
- Cognitive developmental
- Evolutionary
- Learning
- Psychodynamic
- Social cognitive
- Sociocultural

5% Research Strategies and Methodology
- Case study
- Correlational
- Cross-sectional
- Cross sequential
- Experimental
- Longitudinal
- Observational

10% Biological Development Throughout the Life Span
- Development of the brain and nervous system
- Heredity, genetics, and genetic testing
- Hormonal influences
- Influences of drugs
- Motor development
- Nutritional influences
- Perinatal influences
- Physical growth and maturation, aging
- Prenatal influences
- Sexual maturation
- Teratogens

7% Perceptual Development Throughout the Life Span
- Sensitive periods
- Sensorimotor activities
- Sensory acuity
- Sensory deprivation

12% **Cognitive Development Throughout the Life Span**
- Attention
- Environmental influences
- Executive function
- Expertise
- Information processing
- Memory
- Piaget, Jean
- Play
- Problem solving and planning
- Thinking
- Vygotsky, Lev
- Wisdom

8% **Language Development**
- Bilingualism
- Development of syntax
- Environmental, cultural, and genetic influences
- Language and thought
- Pragmatics
- Semantic development
- Vocalization and sound

4% **Intelligence Throughout the Life Span**
- Concepts of intelligence and creativity
- Developmental stability and change
- Heredity and environment

10% **Social Development Throughout the Life Span**
- Aggression
- Attachment
- Gender
- Interpersonal relationships
- Moral development
- Prosocial behavior
- Risk and resilience
- Self
- Social cognition
- Wellness

8% **Family, Home, and Society Throughout the Life Span**
- Abuse and neglect
- Bronfenbrenner, Urie
- Death and dying
- Family relationships
- Family structures
- Media and technology
- Multicultural perspectives
- Parenting styles
- Social and class influences

8% **Personality and Emotion**
- Attribution styles
- Development of emotions
- Emotional expression and regulation
- Emotional intelligence
- Erikson, Erik
- Freud, Sigmund
- Stability and change
- Temperament

8% **Learning**
- Classical conditioning
- Discrimination and generalization
- Habituation
- Operant conditioning
- Social learning and modeling

5% **Schooling, Work, and Interventions**
- Applications of developmental principles
- Facilitation of role transitions
- Intervention programs and services
- Learning styles
- Occupational development
- Preschool care, day care, and elder care
- Retirement

5% **Atypical Development**

- Antisocial behavior
- Asocial behavior, fears, phobias, and obsessions
- Attention-deficit/hyperactivity disorder
- Autism spectrum disorders
- Chronic illnesses and physical disabilities
- Cognitive disorders, including dementia
- Genetic disorders
- Giftedness
- Learning disabilities
- Intellectual Disability
- Mood disorders
- Trauma-based syndromes

SAMPLE TEST

DIRECTIONS: Read each item and select the best response.

1. **Among the choices below, what is the earliest sign that infants are engaging an adult in a mutually reinforcing social interaction?**

   A. Displaying a social smile to an adult

   B. Crying if left in an unfamiliar place by an adult

   C. Playing peek-a-boo with an adult

   D. Trusting an adult stranger to hold them

   E. Expressing disgust after tasting an unpalatable food offering from an adult

2. **Parents decides to ignore the recently occurring and frequent tantrums their two-year-old boy throws whenever they attempt to put on the child's shoes. After about a week the child no longer throws a tantrum when a parent puts on his shoes. According to the theory of operant conditioning, this scenario is a demonstration of**

   A. Sensory deprivation

   B. Negative reinforcement

   C. Extinction

   D. A conditioned response

   E. habituation

3. **What is an indication that a child is not ready for toilet training?**

   A. child has an automatic "no" response to every request

   B. child does not have regular bowel movements at night

   C. child has habitual finger-sucking behavior

   D. child has an older sibling who is not toilet trained

   E. child is less than 26 months of age

4. **What finding in a child warrants an immediate medical evaluation for autism?**

   A. No babbling or baby talk by 12 months of age

   B. No use of toys in creative ways by 24 months of age

   C. Refuses to be held at 24 months of age

   D. Screams when spoken to after 12 months of age

   E. Engages in back-and-forth gestures such as pointing or waving after 9 months of age

5. Katy is a 4th grade student who has received excellent grades in all of her classes except for math. She does well on homework assignments and claims she understands the course material well. She reports that she has trouble sleeping the night before a math test and has" butterflies" before the exam. She has trouble concentrating during the exam. Her math test grades this year are all "Cs". Her overall non-math GPA is 3.7 for this year and the past three years. Which of the statements below is most likely true for Kati?

A. her performance is not likely to improve without individual math tutoring

B. she would perform better if she had an older brother who was a good math student

C. she would perform better if her math instructors were female

D. she probably feels the same before any test, but does not realize this

E. she would perform better on math tests if immediately before the test, she wrote a paragraph or two about her feelings

6. The concrete operational stage is described in which theory of cognitive development?

A. Robbie Case's theory

B. Piaget's theory

C. Vygotsky's theory

D. Information processing theory

E. Kurt Fisher's theory

7. Studies have shown that vocabulary knowledge in children

A. Improves with increased socioeconomic status

B. Is independent of the number of words per hour heard at home

C. Improves with increasing birth order

D. Does not correlate with school failure rates in boys

E. Correlates most strongly with parental ethnicity

8. **Which of the choices below is an example of a cross-sectional study?**

   A. A study analyses data from a single standardized test administered on the same day to all 3rd graders in a school district

   B. A study compares average standardized test scores for students in each grade level of a K-6 elementary school for a specific school year with another specific school year

   C. A study collects and analyzes IQ scores of a group of students throughout their elementary school careers

   D. A study compares percentile distribution scores for all high school students in a single school district taking the ACT in a specific year to percentile distribution scores of all students taking the SAT in the same year and in the same school district.

   E. A study compares the GPAs of all 5th grade white children to the GPAs of all 5th grade non-white children in a school district over the past ten years.

9. **Children go through age-specific time ranges where they must easily acquire knowledge in a specific fashion. What is the term for these ranges of time?**

   A. Transformation ranges

   B. Encoding stages

   C. Metacognitive timeframes

   D. Sensitive periods

   E. Phoneme acquisition stages

10. **In psychoanalytic theory, what is the only personality structure component or stage that is present at birth?**

   A. Sensorimotor stage

   B. Concrete operational stage

   C. The id

   D. Preoperational stage

   E. The ego

11. A teacher institutes the principles of operant conditioning to change a student's undesirable behavior to a new and more desirable behavior. Which of the positive reinforcement schedules shown below is most likely to result in a permanent change in the undesired behavior to the desired behavior?

A. Immediately reward the behavior every time it occurs

B. Immediately reward the behavior every third time it occurs

C. Immediately but variably reward the behavior on an average of every fifth time it occurs

D. Reward the behavior every time it occurs after a brief waiting period

E. Reward the behavior every third time it occurs after a brief waiting period

12. Harry Harlow's experiments with wire mesh and cloth-clad surrogate mothers for infant monkeys showed that infant monkeys spent a greater amount of time with

A. Wire mesh surrogates that provided a source of nourishment over any cloth-clad surrogates that did not provide a source of nourishment

B. Surrogates that provided an electrical source of heat over any other surrogates

C. Any cloth-clad surrogates over any wire mesh surrogates

D. Any surrogate that provided both nourishment and warmth over any surrogate that provide neither nourishment nor warmth

E. Wire mesh surrogates that provided both nourishment and warmth over cloth-clad surrogates that provide nourishment only

13. **Which of the following is a description of the Moro reflex?**

   A. A newborn infant flexes his big toe upward when the lateral side of the foot is rubbed with a blunt instrument

   B. A newborn infant automatically turns its face towards anything that strokes its cheek or mouth

   C. A 4-month-old infant responds to a sudden loss of physical support by first throwing its arms out, then bringing her arms back to her body and then begins to cry.

   D. A 3-month-old infant swings its head and torso toward a stroke along one side of its back

   E. A newborn infant flexes his big toe downward when the lateral side of the foot is rubbed with a blunt instrument

14. **What type of problem is represented by this riddle? Three men need to cross from one side of a river to the other. Two of the men weigh 100 lbs. each and one man weighs 200 lbs. The boat they use to cross can carry no more than 200 lbs. at one time. How do the men all cross to the other side of the river?**

   A. Analogy

   B. Experimental

   C. Classification

   D. Heuristic

   E. transformation

15. **Which of the following statements is true regarding an autosomal dominant trait?**

   A. Children with the trait always have at least one parent with the trait

   B. Children with the trait may have both parents who do not have the trait

   C. If both parents have the trait there is a 50% chance their children will have the trait

   D. If at least one parent has the trait, all of the children will have the trait

   E. If both parents have the trait, all of the children will have the trait

16. **The memory process of encoding**

   A. Is the first step in memory retrieval

   B. Occurs primarily during REM stage sleep

   C. Allows conversion of verbal memories into visual imagery

   D. Begins with a sensory perception

   E. Is the last step in memory consolidation

17. **A decrease in the production of what hormone begins the process of menopause in women?**

    A. Aldosterone

    B. Progesterone

    C. Estrogen

    D. cortisol

    E. testosterone

18. **Which stage of development is not included in Jean Piaget's theory of cognitive development?**

    A. Postformal thought

    B. Formal operations

    C. Concrete operations

    D. Sensorimotor

    E. Pre-operational

19. **Teresa is a 31-year-old woman who is seeing a psychoanalytic therapist. The therapy sessions are currently focusing on Teresa's tendency to choose intimate male partners who possess traits that she finds similarity to those of her father. The therapist would most likely explain this tendency in terms of**

    A. Anaclitic object choice

    B. Erotogenicity

    C. Transference

    D. Counter-transference

    E. Ego cathexis

20. **In cognitive psychology, what is the term applied to the proposed mechanism of language acquisition where children are able to generate a new hypothesis based on even one single exposure to a unit of information?**

    A. Referent selection

    B. Associative proposal

    C. Whole-object bias

    D. Cross situational learning

    E. Fast mapping

21. **In James Marcia's identity status theory, which statement below represents the adolescent stage of identity foreclosure?**

    A. "I am going to be a fireman because my father was a fireman."

    B. "I believe in God, but I am going to investigate a wide range of religions to determine which feels right for me"

    C. "I don't really fit in with any of the social cliques at my high school, and that's fine with me"

    D. "I refuse to change who I am regardless of anyone else's opinion"

    E. "I sometimes wonder if I really have any identity at all"

22. **Theorist Lev Vygotsky proposes that social interactions**

    A. Require higher-level cognitive functionality

    B. Occur in children only after they attain identity stability

    C. Play a fundamental role is the development of human cognition

    D. Are based on behavioral tendencies that are present at birth

    E. Interfere with objective awareness of existential threats

23. **A retrospective study on residents in a Japanese fishing village showed that severe neurological damage occurred in many villagers during a specific time span. Researchers were able to use the study data to identify the agent that caused the neurological damage, an organic form of the heavy metal mercury. Study data also showed a direct, strong correlation between the level of severity of neurological damage in subjects of the study and the total amount of fish consumed from the bay of the village during a critical time span by subjects of the study. In this study, the level of neurological damage was the**

    A. Cohort

    B. Dependent variable

    C. Independent variable

    D. Controlled variable

    E. correlation coefficient

24. A researcher conducted a study of a population of South Pacific Islanders and concluded, based on structured interviews, that the islanders, as a single ethnic group, had a much higher rate of acceptance of promiscuity and infidelity compared to other ethnic groups. Researchers later discovered that the islanders actually view promiscuity and infidelity at least as unfavorably as other ethnic groups, and that they, as a group, had conspired to provide the opposite impression to the original researcher as an elaborate practical joke. The erroneous conclusion in the original study represents

A. An inadequate methodology

B. A cultural bias of the researcher

C. A failure to provide a control group

D. A failure to replicate the original study before reaching a conclusion

E. A selection bias

25. Some females are born with condition called mosaic Turner syndrome, where some of their cells have only one X chromosome and the other cells have two X chromosomes. If 50% of a female's cells have only one X chromosome. At what stage of prenatal development did the chromosomal abnormality likely first occur?

A. Before ovulation

B. During ovulation

C. After ovulation and before fertilization

D. At the zygote stage

E. After the zygote stage but before the fetal stage

26. The Tanner scale is used to evaluate which of the following?

A. External primary and secondary sex characteristics

B. Stages of formal operations

C. Emotional levels of maturity

D. Levels of memory impairment

E. Maturity levels of motor functioning

27. A toddler is about to probe an electrical wall socket with a metal fork. As he moves the fork forward, he glances back at his mother and observes the mother displaying facial expression of extreme fear and disapproval. In response, the toddler withdraws the fork and looks for other forms of entertainment. The toddler during this scenario is demonstrating

A. Social modeling

B. An unconditioned response

C. Social referencing

D. Self-preservation

E. Mirroring

28. A 39-year-old woman is in her 12th week of pregnancy. Her obstetrician has recommended that she undergo chorionic villus sampling. What is the purpose of this test?

A. To test for chromosomal or genetic abnormalities of the fetus

B. To determine if the fetus is at a normal developmental stage

C. To determine if the mother has a different Rh blood type than the fetus

D. To determine if the fetus has an adequate umbilical blood supply

E. To test for abnormalities in the amniotic fluid surrounding the fetus.

29. In studies comparing the shared expression of traits between monozygotic twins raised in the same household vs. those raised in separate households, which trait should show the least environmental influence on its expression?

A. Eye color

B. Male pattern baldness

C. Adult height

D. Intelligence

E. Skin tone

30. Researchers have demonstrated that infants are capable of integrating information acquired simultaneously through at least two different senses. This ability to transfer learning from one sense to another is referred to as

A. Sensory indexing

B. Synesthesia

C. Immediate consciousness

D. Intermodal perception

E. Multitasking

31. Jennifer is a college senior. She has a few friends and a pleasant though somewhat distant relationship with her close family members. She enjoys spending time with her new boyfriend Jeff. For the first time she has someone she feels comfortable discussing very personal issues with. Jennifer now thinks she knows what qualities she is looking for in a potential husband, and she is discovering that Jeff possesses many of these qualities. Jennifer is most likely in the Erik Erikson's stage of

    A. initiative vs. guilt

    B. industry vs. inferiority

    C. trust vs. mistrust

    D. identity vs. identity confusion

    E. Intimacy vs. isolation

32. Brian is a 50-year-old man who was recently demoted by his work supervisor to a position of significantly lesser authority and monetary compensation. Brian adopts an attitude of "well, things could be worse, I'll get by." According to Hopson's model of transitions, Brian is engaging in

    A. Role blurring

    B. Minimization

    C. Internalization

    D. Derealization

    E. Optimization

33. According to the principles of Social Learning Theory, vicarious reinforcement is occurring in which of the following situations?

    A. A baseball pitcher learns to throw a curveball by watching other pitchers throw curveballs

    B. An actor visualizes an Oscar nomination resulting from successfully reproducing subtle attributes he imagines for a character he is portraying in a film

    C. A student overcomes fear of public speaking by speaking first in front of friends, than to gradually less familiar audiences

    D. A singer increases her vocal range by receiving praise from her voice coach each time she is able to reproduce a note with a pitch slightly outside of her previous range.

    E. A Basketball player modifies his ball-handling style based on spectator reactions to other player's ball-handling styles

34. Erin is a 25-year-old woman who is changing a flat tire for the first time. She is in an extremely hazardous location and must move her vehicle at least one mile uphill to remove herself from this life-threatening situation. The tire has four lug nuts. As Erin mounts a replacement tire, the four lug nuts fall down a steep embankment and are irretrievable. Erin devises a temporary solution for her dilemma by removing one lug nut from each of the other three tires and using the three lug nuts to satisfactorily mount the replacement tire. According to Robert Sternberg's theory, Erin's thought process demonstrates

    A. Risk and resilience

    B. Pragmatism

    C. Prosocial behavior

    D. Role transitioning

    E. High Intelligence

35. Which of the following is an example of an occurrence of semantic under extension?

    A. A child refers to all four-legged creatures as "cats"

    B. A child refers to the family cats as cats but does not refer to other cats as cats

    C. A child refers to a gardener as a "plant-man."

    D. A child assumes the family dog, named Fido, is a "Fido" and refers to all other dogs are "Fidos."

    E. A child states: "I home," meaning "I am at home."

36. In terms of age-normal visual ability, an 8-month-old infant

    A. Cannot focus on objects between eight and 15 inches away

    B. Cannot focus on objects greater than 3 feet away

    C. Cannot discriminate between basic colors

    D. Has limited depth perception

    E. Has normal adult vision

37. **B.F. Skinner's theory of language acquisition proposes that**

    A. Language acquisition occurs by reinforcement.

    B. Children are born with an innate universal grammar ability

    C. Children have an highly refined ability to recognize patterns in language

    D. Children are born with an ability to recognize any phoneme in any language

    E. Acquisition of language occurs by a gradual pattern learning process based on the concept of "morphemes."

38. **An 8-year-old boy has been classified as having a moderate intellectual disability. Based on this classification, which of the following statements is true regarding the child?**

    A. He can learn up to a normal sixth grade level

    B. He has poor social awareness

    C. He has poor motor coordination

    D. He has an IQ between 70 and 90

    E. He has extremely limited cognition

39. **Research has shown that older people tend to have lower IQ scores than younger people. The Flynn effect states that this age related difference in IQ scores is**

    A. Evidence that intelligence decreases with age

    B. Due to a worldwide increase in IQ scores at a rate of 3 points per decade

    C. A consequence of lower motivation to test well in older persons rather than an actual lower average IQ in older persons

    D. A result of a strong correlation between increasing IQ and mortality in World War II.

    E. A statistical failure to renormalize IQ scoring resulting in an IQ score of 110 today being equivalent to an IQ score of 100 in 1940.

40. **Each of the choices below describes a reaction by a young child to the presence of a stranger. Choose the reaction that indicates the highest level of anxiety in the child.**

    A. running to a caregiver

    B. grabbing the caregiver's legs

    C. silence and wariness combined with a fearful facial expression

    D. demanding to be picked up by a caregiver

    E. refusing to look into the eyes of a stranger

41. **In Kohlberg's theory of Cognitive development, modeling the behavior of members of the same sex occurs**

    A. After the realization that the gender of a person does not change

    B. Before the age of three

    C. Only after a child has developed the mental construct of a gender association schema

    D. With a delayed onset in single parent households where the parent is of the opposite sex

    E. As early as the first month of life

42. **Choose the correct order when infants begin to demonstrate the following motor skills from the earliest to the latest age:**

    I. **Rolls from back to side**
    II. **Holds head up when sitting**
    III. **Bears weight on forearms**

    A. I, II, III

    B. III, I, II

    C. II, III, I

    D. I, III, II

    E. III, II, I

43. **In Pavlov's experiments, dogs learned to salivate in response to an auditory cue. In later experiments these dogs began to salivate in response to a different but similar auditory cue. What is the term for this type of new response?**

    A. Operant conditioning

    B. Unconditioned

    C. Discrimination

    D. Sensitization

    E. Generalization

44. **Research has shown children are more likely to have higher IQs on average if they are**

    A. An only child

    B. Female and have an older brother

    C. The second born of three siblings

    D. The second born and have no other siblings

    E. Male and have an at least one older brother

45. **In psychology, what is a general principle that is shared by stage theory and non-stage models of information processing in humans?**

    A. Multiple neuro-anatomical locations of information storage

    B. Two-way flow of information

    C. Serial, discontinuous information processing

    D. Different levels of elaboration during information processing

    E. Lack of a biological predisposition to process information

46. **Among the choices below, which is the recommended method of discouraging undesirable behavior in children based on the principles of operant conditioning?**

    A. Distracting the child while the behavior is occurring

    B. Punishing the behavior on a frequent but unpredictable schedule

    C. Punishing the behavior every time it occurs

    D. Rewarding the child for not engaging in the behavior for a specified period of time

    E. Rewarding the child every time the behavior is voluntarily terminated upon request

47. **Which type of theory proposes that a person can learn to start a fire using only naturally occurring forest resources without first practicing any of the techniques required to achieve this task?**

    A. Social cognitive

    B. Sociocultural

    C. Psychodynamic

    D. Evolutionary

    E. Behavioral

48. A 3-year-old child has been scratched by several different cats. After investigating the family cat's paws, he discovers they contain sharp claws. The child concludes all cats can probably scratch him. What cognitive ability did the child use to reach this conclusion?

A. Deductive reasoning

B. Inductive reasoning

C. Abductive reasoning

D. Conjectural reasoning

E. Suppositional reasoning

49. According to John Holland's theory, which personality type prefers physical jobs that involve skill strength and coordination?

A. Enterprising

B. Social

C. Realistic

D. Conventional

E. Artistic

50. What field of knowledge addresses the ambiguity in the statement "I saw the room with a telescope?"

A. Etymology

B. Symbolics

C. Semantics

D. Pragmatics

E. Lexicology

51. Severe, progressive memory loss is most characteristic of which of the following conditions?

A. Down's syndrome (trisomy 13)

B. Autism

C. Parkinson's disease

D. Lou Gehrig's disease (ALS)

E. Alzheimer's disease

52. According to Elisabeth Kübler-Ross' theory, adults who erroneously believe that they could have taken actions to directly prevent the recent death of a loved one are in which stage of grief?

A. Retrospective

B. Denial

C. Imaginary

D. Bargaining

E. Depression

53. **What is one of the major criticisms of Piaget's principles in his theory of learning?**

   A. Very young children are markedly involved in egocentric speech

   B. Research studies have shown that children can learn particular concepts before they reach prerequisite stages

   C. Other cultures have a high regard for scientific thinking

   D. Children can understand the conservation of weight and the conservation of number at the same operational stage

   E. On average, boys are able to learn particular concepts at a younger age than girls

54. **Which theorist describes the concept of the "zone of proximal development"?**

   A. Erik Erikson

   B. Jean Piaget

   C. John Holland

   D. Lev Vygotsky

   E. Robert Sternberg

55. **In behaviorist theory, habituation is occurring in which of the following scenarios?**

   A. A wife experiences increasingly strong desires for alcohol intake each succeeding night that her husband arrives home late from work

   B. Over a several month period, a child takes less time to finish a particular chore in response to his mother's constant nagging.

   C. Over time a man is able to fall asleep more easily despite the continuous nightly barking of a neighbor's dog just outside the man's bedroom window

   D. When an attractive girl smiles at a boy every time he rubs his nose, over time the boy begins to rub his nose each time the girl smiles at him

   E. A drug addict experiences increased cravings for a drug even though he is increasing the frequency that he uses the drug.

56. In terms of age, from earliest to latest, in what order do children typically acquire the grammatical morphemes?

   I. Regular plural – s (dog – dogs)
   II. Possessive – s (Mom – Mom's)
   III. Present progressive – ing (walk – walking)

   A. I, II, III

   B. II, I, III

   C. III, II, I

   D. I, III, II

   E. III, I, II

57. Robert Sternberg's triangle theory describes three components of

   A. Language acquisition

   B. Moral development

   C. Adult love

   D. Faith development

   E. Object relations

58. Stavros is a United States born, 35-year-old son of ethnic Greek immigrant parents. He is successful and happily married. He began to identify himself as ethnically Greek in his early teenage years. Today his ethnic heritage is a source of pride and this ethnic image of himself plays a major role in most aspects of his life. According to social theory, Stavros' ethnic identity

   A. May have replaced an earlier negative ethnic self-image

   B. Probably includes an exaggerated sense of importance of Greek culture within the overall culture of the United States

   C. Represents an internalization of his ethnicity

   D. Probably serves to mask significant insecurity issues related to his ethnic minority status

   E. Is very likely to play a diminishing role in his choice of social activities as he gets older

59. In what age range is the initial diagnosis of schizophrenia most common?

   A. Between 10 and 24 years

   B. Between 16 and 30 years

   C. Between 25 and 40 years

   D. Between 45 and 59 years

   E. After age 60 years

60. A research study follows 100 children with a history of lead exposure for a 10-year period. They each are administered three separate standardized tests each year. The results are compared to score distribution curves for the tests results of all children of the same age nationwide who took the tests in the same years. What is the cohort in this study?

   A. Lead exposure

   B. The group of 100 children

   C. The three standardized tests

   D. The 10-year period

   E. The nationwide test score distribution curves

61. A young child who is using telegraphic speech is

   A. Using one word to function as a full sentence

   B. Compressing a grammatically correct statement into a two-word statement lacking conjunctions or articles

   C. Speaking with an exaggerated tone and rhythm

   D. Speaking softly in a manner not directed at or intended for others to hear

   E. Verbally conveying a thought that is intelligible and grammatically correct

62. Which researcher's work has shown that newborns younger than 8 months appear to have an innate ability to universally distinguish all fundamentally unique speech sounds, and that this ability is not present in adults who are learning a new language?

   A. Noam Chomsky

   B. Anne Fernald

   C. Jenny Saffran

   D. Richard Montague

   E. Janet Werker

63. According to Lawrence Kolberg's theory, a teenage that arrives at a moral judgment of an act by considering the social consequences of the act is in what stage of moral development?

   A. Pre-conventional

   B. conventional

   C. post-conventional

   D. empirical

   E. transcendental

64. **Researchers using data collected from a study find there is a linear relationship between two variables. If the correlation coefficient (r) is calculated from a graph plot of the data, which of the correlation coefficient values shown below would indicate the strongest relationship between the two variables?**

   A. 0.2

   B. -0.9

   C. 0.5

   D. -0.1

   E. 0.0

65. **Mildred Parten's theory and classification of play participation in children describes activities that are interactive but lacking in formal rules or organization as**

   A. Parallel play

   B. Independent play

   C. Associative play

   D. Immature play

   E. Chaotic play

66. **According to psychological theories of cognitive development, which of the following tasks requires the highest level of executive function?**

   A. Selecting the most qualified persons to fill management positions in a company

   B. Accurately predicting trends in emerging markets

   C. Developing strong interpersonal relationships with important business clients

   D. Providing persuasive testimony in support of desirable regulatory legislation

   E. Devising novel, focused adaptations to a complex, rapidly changing business environment

67. **What is a valid evolutionary explanation for the relative success of societies that place a high value on the contributions of their elderly citizens to the well-being of the society?**

   A. There is a very small percentage of elderly persons in such societies

   B. Insufficient time has passed for evolutionary process to have selected out these societies

   C. Such societies are geographically isolated from other societies.

   D. The elderly in these societies provide information and services that increase the likelihood that children will survive and produce viable offspring

   E. An individual's longevity is correlated with high reproductive success during the individual's fertile years.

68. **Research has shown that the divorce rate in the United States is**

   A. Lower for couples who both have a 4-year college degree compared to those with only a high school degree

   B. Lower for second marriages compared to first marriages

   C. Lower for Black couples than Hispanic couples

   D. Lower in couples who cohabitate before marriage compared to couples who do not cohabitate before marriage

   E. Lower for couples who marry at a young age compared to couples who marry later in life

69. **In infants who are exclusively breast-fed beyond the age of six months, which nutrient is not provided is sufficient amounts?**

   A. Vitamin A

   B. Protein

   C. Riboflavin

   D. Vitamin B-12

   E. Iron

70. **Which of the following cognitive skills does not normally decline in an individual as a result of aging?**

    A. Fluid intelligence

    B. Recall of recent events

    C. Divided attention

    D. Vocabulary

    E. Word retrieval

71. **Miranda is an 18-year-old woman who has an overwhelming fear of spiders. A clinical psychologist has recommended that Amanda undergo a course of aversion therapy in order to overcome this abnormal level of fear. What is the theoretical basis for this form of therapy?**

    A. Operant conditioning

    B. Classical conditioning

    C. Principles of psychoanalysis

    D. Principles of social cognition

    E. Principles of Socratic methodology

72. **Ingrid is a young woman who has completed a Big Five standardized personality inventory questionnaire. She scores highly in one of the five personality dimensions indicating she strongly prefers planned behaviors over spontaneous behaviors. What personality dimension is this?**

    A. Openness to experience

    B. Conscientiousness

    C. Extraversion

    D. Agreeableness

    E. Neuroticism

73. **Deborah is a private tutor for a 5th grade student, Rick, who is having difficulty with the task of determining the slope of a line from a graph. Deborah's teaching method begins with choosing an interesting graphing task and then guiding Rick in a step by step fashion through the process of plotting data on a graph and then obtaining the slope of the resulting line. Successive lessons involve less input by Deborah until Rick is able to determine the slope of a line without Deborah's assistance. What is the term for this learning process?**

    A. Cognitive guidance

    B. Instructional scaffolding

    C. Semiotic instruction

    D. Pedagogy

    E. Inquiry learning

74. **Peyton is a 17-year-old girl who has never had a menstrual period. A physical examination the previous year showed no physical abnormalities. Among the choices below what is an important possible explanation for Peyton's delayed menarche?**

    A. Undiagnosed herpes simplex infection

    B. Excessive dietary iron intake

    C. Food allergies

    D. Pregnancy

    E. Lack of physical exercise

75. **Bevan is a 15-year-old boy who emigrated to the United States with his biological parents 12 years ago. Bevan has maintained a 4.0 grade point average throughout his elementary and high school career. His teachers all agree that Bevan has always been exceptionally motivated to perform well in school. Among the choices below, which is most likely to account for Bevan's high motivation to achieve academic success?**

    A. Both parents have high IQs

    B. A higher socioeconomic status compared to most other student's households.

    C. High resiliency due to exposure to significant but manageable environmental stress at a young age.

    D. A compensatory response to perceived ethno-cultural prejudice

    E. A cultural background that emphasizes the importance of academic achievement

76. **Vertigo that is not caused by an abnormality occurring inside the brain is most likely to be caused by**

    A. Abnormal functioning of the semicircular canals

    B. Damage to the retina

    C. Abnormal hormone levels

    D. Damage to a large peripheral motor nerve

    E. Small nerve damage in patients with diabetes

77. **Paul, a 10-year-old boy, has observed that another student at school, Tim, is the object of ridicule by a clique of peers that Paul considers to be "the cool kids". Paul decides to punch Tim in the face. If Paul's decision was motivated by the fact that the "in crowd "clique was sure to witness his assault on Tim, Paul's behavior is most likely an example of**

    A. Passive-aggressive behavior

    B. Instrumental aggression

    C. Scapegoating

    D. Dehumanization

    E. Subservience

78. **A young boy observes that his father always mows the lawn and that his mother always does the laundry. From these observations and others in the outside world he has concluded that men are physically strong and women are comparatively physically weak. Over time the boy develops a mental catalogue of this and other gender related connections. In gender schema theory, this mental framework**

    A. Is required to allow the boy to assign himself a gender

    B. Leads to the recognition that gender is constant throughout life

    C. Provides a mechanism to evaluate discrepancies observed in gender based behavior in other individuals

    D. Influences judgments about behavior and promotes gender stereotyping

    E. Is an example of generalized behavior pattern seen in most mammals that live in herds or other extended groups

79. What theorist proposed an explanation of personality based on conscious forces and unconscious desires and beliefs?

    A. Sigmund Freud

    B. Jean Piaget

    C. Hans Jürgen Eysenck

    D. Raymond Cattell

    E. Urie Bronfenbrenner

80. Beginning around the age of three to four months, what is most likely to elicit laughter from a child?

    A. Actions that involve another child close to their own age

    B. Interactions with a household pet

    C. Interactions with caregivers that deviate from normal interactions

    D. Actions that result in laughter from a caregiver

    E. Interactions that occur in a group activity of three or more persons including the child

81. Akihiro's native language is Japanese. He is twenty-five years old and began learning English five years ago. He has achieved professional working fluency in English, but tests conducted by a linguistic audiologist confirms he is unable to detect the difference between the English "L" and "R" sounds. For example, the words "lent" and "rent" sound the same to him. This is an example of

    A. Aphonia

    B. Echolalia

    C. Categorical perception

    D. Dyslexia

    E. Atonic dissonance

82. Sarah is an 8-year-old girl who was born with a group of characteristic abnormal facial features. Her development of many gross and fine motor skills occurred at a significantly later age than normal. She suffers from mental retardation, impaired language development and seizures. During Sarah's prenatal development, which of the factors described below is the most likely explanation for her condition?

A. Inadequate thiamine intake by the mother

B. Heavy alcohol use by the mother

C. Heavy marijuana use by the mother

D. Undiagnosed diabetes in the mother

E. Heavy cigarette smoking by the mother

83. Margaret is a 40-year-old independent consultant who was recently hired by a large company because of Margaret's track record of utilizing multiple highly effective strategies to provide solutions to companies who were experiencing serious, complex and unexpected problems. Margaret's value to her clients, in psychological terms, is her

A. Altruism

B. Pragmatism

C. Wisdom

D. Expertise

E. Resilience

84. **In Psychology, risk and resiliency theories would most likely propose a mechanism to explain which of the following observations?**

    A. In a controlled situation, a driver demonstrates lower than expected impairment of driving skills while under the influence of alcohol

    B. Some employees are able to perform tasks exceptionally well in a rapidly changing work environment

    C. Teenagers sharing certain types of interpersonal relationships are less likely to engage in drug use

    D. An undesirable behavior continues to recur despite repeated application of negative reinforcement schedules

    E. A religious practice among a group persists despite decades of repression by a government

85. **A 50-year-old woman has end-stage pancreatic cancer. Her physicians have recommended her transfer to a facility that will provide care and treatment that provide comfort but no further treatment that is designed to alter the course of her disease. In the United States, what is the term for this type of care?**

    A. Custodial

    B. Minimal

    C. Euthanasia

    D. supportive

    E. Hospice

86. **In substance abuse and compulsive behavior intervention programs, which of the following encourage the subject of the intervention to adopt a set of guiding principles?**

    A. Twelve-step programs

    B. Paradoxical intervention programs

    C. Primal therapy programs

    D. Transference interpretation programs

    E. Behavioral therapy intervention programs

87. **Critics of evolutionary theories of social behavior claim certain prosocial behaviors cannot be explained based on the principles of evolution. Which of the following is an example of this type of prosocial behavior?**

    A. Altruism

    B. Nepotism

    C. Cooperativism

    D. Commensalism

    E. hedonism

88. **Jerry is a 30-year-old man who is interviewing for a job. During the interview, Jerry engages in subconscious behavior to build rapport with the interviewer. Jerry is most likely**

    A. Misdirecting

    B. patronizing

    C. Mirroring

    D. Supplicating

    E. Soliciting

89. **Douglas is a 26-year-old man who is widely regarded by his family and friends as a person with a very optimistic attitude. Whenever Doug experiences a negative event in his life he is more likely to attribute the cause of the event to**

    A. Random chance instead of a specific cause

    B. An error on his part instead of someone else's

    C. A spiritual rather than a naturalistic cause

    D. A temporary set of external circumstances rather than a permanent external condition

    E. Unavoidable external rather than avoidable external circumstances

90. **Martin is a normal, healthy 5-year-old boy who has always been in the 60th percentile of height and weight for boys his age. Assuming Martin has a typical childhood environment and upbringing, with no significant health or psychiatric issues, what would be his least likely height vs. weight percentiles at age 18?**

   A. 60th percentile for height vs. 60th percentile for weight

   B. 60th percentile for height vs. 50th percentile for weight

   C. 70th percentile for height vs. 70th percentile for weight

   D. 70th percentile for height vs. 50th percentile for weight

   E. 80th percentile for height vs. 70th percentile for weight.

ANSWER KEY

Question Number	Correct Answer	Your Answer	Question Number	Correct Answer	Your Answer	Question Number	Correct Answer	Your Answer
1	A		31	E		61	B	
2	C		32	B		62	E	
3	B		33	E		63	B	
4	A		34	E		64	B	
5	E		35	B		65	C	
6	B		36	D		66	E	
7	A		37	A		67	D	
8	A		38	B		68	A	
9	D		39	B		69	E	
10	C		40	C		70	D	
11	C		41	A		71	B	
12	C		42	B		72	C	
13	C		43	E		73	B	
14	E		44	A		74	D	
15	A		45	C		75	E	
16	D		46	C		76	A	
17	C		47	A		77	B	
18	A		48	B		78	D	
19	A		49	C		79	A	
20	E		50	D		80	C	
21	A		51	E		81	C	
22	C		52	D		82	B	
23	B		53	B		83	D	
24	A		54	D		84	C	
25	E		55	C		85	E	
26	A		56	E		86	A	
27	C		57	C		87	A	
28	A		58	A		88	C	
29	A		59	B		89	D	
30	D		60	B		90	D	

RATIONALES

1. **Among the choices below, what is the earliest sign that infants are engaging an adult in a mutually reinforcing social interaction?**

    A. Displaying a social smile to an adult

    B. Crying if left in an unfamiliar place by an adult

    C. Playing peek-a-boo with an adult

    D. Trusting an adult stranger to hold them

    E. Expressing disgust after tasting an unpalatable food offering from an adult

The answer is A.
One of the earliest signs of emotional expressivity in infants is the display of a social smile. The smile is directed at adults and is reinforced by a positive response from the adult. This creates a cycle of mutually positive feedback that results in a pleasant social interaction.

2. **Parents decides to ignore the recently occurring and frequent tantrums their two-year-old boy throws whenever they attempt to put on the child's shoes. After about a week the child no longer throws a tantrum when a parent puts on his shoes. According to the theory of operant conditioning, this scenario is a demonstration of**

    A. Sensory deprivation

    B. Negative reinforcement

    C. Extinction

    D. A conditioned response

    E. habituation

The answer is C.
In operant conditioning theory, extinction is the elimination of a behavior by withholding any form of reinforcement in repose to the behavior. It is important to withhold reinforcement every time the behavior occurs, otherwise all progress in eliminating the behavior will be lost and the extinction schedule must begin anew.

3.   **What is an indication that a child is not ready for toilet training?**

   A.   child has an automatic "no" response to every request

   B.   child does not have regular bowel movements at night

   C.   child has habitual finger-sucking behavior

   D.   child has an older sibling who is not toilet trained

   E.   child is less than 26 months of age

The answer is B.
Children who do not want to use the toilet and/or are unwilling to cooperate with their caregivers are generally not emotionally ready to begin toilet training.   The automatic "no" response to every request stage is an indication that toilet training attempts will not go well.

4.   **What finding in a child warrants an immediate medical evaluation for autism?**

   A.   No babbling or baby talk by 12 months of age

   B.   No use of toys in creative ways by 24 months of age

   C.   Refuses to be held at 24 months of age

   D.   Screams when spoken to after 12 months of age

   E.   Engages in back-and-forth gestures such as pointing or waving after 9 months of age

The answer is A.
There are five specific developmental delays occurring between 6 and 24 months of age that warrant immediate evaluation for autism. No babbling or baby talk by 12 months of age is one of these five red flags.

5. Katy is a 4th grade student who has received excellent grades in all of her classes except for math. She does well on homework assignments and claims she understands the course material well. She reports that she has trouble sleeping the night before a math test and has" butterflies" before the exam. She has trouble concentrating during the exam. Her math test grades this year are all "Cs".Her overall non-math GPA is 3.7 for this year and the past three years. Which of the statements below is most likely true for Kati?

   A. her performance is not likely to improve without individual math tutoring

   B. she would perform better if she had an older brother who was a good math student

   C. she would perform better if her math instructors were female

   D. she probably feels the same before any test, but does not realize this.

   E. she would perform better on math tests if immediately before the test, she wrote a paragraph or two about her feelings

The answer is E.
Large well-conducted research studies have shown that students with math anxiety who write about their feelings immediately before a test perform better than those who do not.

6. **The concrete operational stage is described in which theory of cognitive development?**

   A. Robbie Case's theory

   B. Piaget's theory

   C. Vygotsky's theory

   D. Information processing theory

   E. Kurt Fisher's theory

The answer is B.
Piaget's theory of cognitive development describes four stages. The concrete operational stage usually occurs in children ages 7 to 11 years, where they demonstrate concrete, logical reasoning.

7.   **Studies have shown that vocabulary knowledge in children**

    A. Improves with increased socioeconomic status

    B. Is independent of the number of words per hour heard at home

    C. Improves with increasing birth order

    D. Does not correlate with school failure rates in boys

    E. Correlates most strongly with parental ethnicity

The answer is A.
Studies show that there is a gap in vocabulary knowledge between children raised in economically disadvantaged households compared to economically advantaged households. Lower vocabulary knowledge correlates with poor academic performance.

8.   **Which of the choices below is an example of a cross-sectional study?**

    A. A study analyses data from a single standardized test administered on the same day to all 3rd graders in a school district

    B. A study compares average standardized test scores for students in each grade level of a K-6 elementary school for a specific school year with another specific school year

    C. A study collects and analyzes IQ scores of a group of students throughout their elementary school careers

    D. A study compares percentile distribution scores for all high school students in a single school district taking the ACT in a specific year to percentile distribution scores of all students taking the SAT in the same year and in the same school district.

    E. A study compares the GPAs of all 5th grade white children to the GPAs of all 5th grade non-white children in a school district over the past ten years.

The answer is A.
Cross-sectional studies involve the analysis of data obtained at a specific time from a specific population.

9. **Children go through age-specific time ranges where they most easily acquire knowledge in a specific fashion. What is the term for these ranges of time?**

    A. Transformation ranges

    B. Encoding stages

    C. Metacognitive timeframes

    D. Sensitive periods

    E. Phoneme acquisition stages

The answer is D.
Geneticist Hugo De Vries and educator Maria Montessori most prominently promoted the term "sensitive periods" to refer to age-specific time ranges where children most easily acquire knowledge in a specific way. These phases are characterized by observable behaviors and most occur before the age of six.

10. **In psychoanalytic theory, what is the only personality structure component or stage that is present at birth?**

    A. Sensorimotor stage

    B. Concrete operational stage

    C. The id

    D. Preoperational stage

    E. The ego

The answer is C.
In psychoanalytic theory, there are three major components that interact to generate a complex personality: the id, the ego and the super-ego. The id is the only personality structure component that is present at birth. The id is the repository of instinctive drive states and is the source of desires for immediate gratification.

11. **A teacher institutes the principles of operant conditioning to change a student's undesirable behavior to a new and more desirable behavior. Which of the positive reinforcement schedules shown below is most likely to result in a permanent change in the undesired behavior to the desired behavior?**

    A. Immediately reward the behavior every time it occurs

    B. Immediately reward the behavior every third time it occurs

    C. Immediately but variably reward the behavior on an average of every fifth time it occurs

    D. Reward the behavior every time it occurs after a brief waiting period

    E. Reward the behavior every third time it occurs after a brief waiting period

The answer is C.
All of the choices except choice "C" are fixed reward schedules. Fixed reward schedules are effective in teaching a behavior change, but the original behavior tends to recur soon after the reward schedule is discontinued. Choice "C" is a variable reward schedule, with an uncertain reward provided in any single instance when the behavior change is performed. Variable reward schedules are more likely to produce behavior changes that persist even after the reward schedule is discontinued.

12. **Harry Harlow's experiments with wire mesh and cloth-clad surrogate mothers for infant monkeys showed that infant monkeys spent a greater amount of time with**

   A. Wire mesh surrogates that provided a source of nourishment over any cloth-clad surrogates that did not provide a source of nourishment

   B. Surrogates that provided an electrical source of heat over any other surrogates

   C. Any cloth-clad surrogates over any wire mesh surrogates

   D. Any surrogate that provided both nourishment and warmth over any surrogate that provide neither nourishment nor warmth

   E. Wire mesh surrogates that provided both nourishment and warmth over cloth-clad surrogates that provide nourishment only

The answer is C.
Harlow's study found that infant monkeys always spent a greater amount of time with soft, cloth-clad surrogate mothers over sharp-edged wire mesh mothers, regardless of whether the wire mesh surrogates provided food and/or water. All of the motherless infants exhibited strange behavior during the study. As adults, the females showed negligence and abuse toward their infant offspring.

13. **Which of the following is a description of the Moro reflex?**

   A. A newborn infant flexes his big toe upward when the lateral side of the foot is rubbed with a blunt instrument

   B. A newborn infant automatically turns its face towards anything that strokes its cheek or mouth

   C. A 4-month-old infant responds to a sudden loss of physical support by first throwing its arms out, then bringing her arms back to her body and then begins to cry.

   D. A 3-month-old infant swings its head and torso toward a stroke along one side of its back

   E. A newborn infant flexes his big toe downward when the lateral side of the foot is rubbed with a blunt instrument

The answer is C.
The Moro reflex is normally present in infants of age 4 to 5 months. In response to a sudden lack of support, which presumably creates a falling sensation, infants throw their arms out (abduction) then bring their arms in (adduction), then begin to cry.

14. **What type of problem is represented by this riddle? Three men need to cross from one side of a river to the other. Two of the men weigh 100 lbs. each and one man weighs 200 lbs. The boat they use to cross can carry no more than 200 lbs. at one time. How do the men all cross to the other side of the river?**

   A. Analogy

   B. Experimental

   C. Classification

   D. Heuristic

   E. transformation

The answer is E.
Transformation problems require a series of changes to achieve a specific goal. In this case multiple river crossings are required, and each crossing requires changes in the personnel that occupy the boat

15. **Which of the following statements is true regarding an autosomal dominant trait?**

   A. Children with the trait always have at least one parent with the trait

   B. Children with the trait may have both parents who do not have the trait

   C. If both parents have the trait there is a 50% chance their children will have the trait

   D. If at least one parent has the trait, all of the children will have the trait

   E. If both parents have the trait, all of the children will have the trait

The answer is A.
An autosomal dominant trait is always expressed. If neither parent has the trait then the trait is not present in either parent and therefore cannot be passed on to their offspring.

16. **The memory process of encoding**

    A. Is the first step in memory retrieval

    B. Occurs primarily during REM stage sleep

    C. Allows conversion of verbal memories into visual imagery

    D. Begins with a sensory perception

    E. Is the last step in memory consolidation

The answer is D.
Encoding is the first step in memory creation. Encoding first requires a perception acquired through the senses; sight, sound etc. to begin forming and storing a specific memory

17. **A decrease in the production of what hormone begins the process of menopause in women?**

    A. Aldosterone

    B. Progesterone

    C. Estrogen

    D. cortisol

    E. testosterone

The answer is C.
Menopause in women begins when their ovaries decrease their production of estrogen. The levels of other hormones may also change during and after menopause, but it is the decrease in estrogen that directly or indirectly leads to changes in other hormone levels.

18. **Which stage of development is not included in Jean Piaget's theory of cognitive development?**

    A. Postformal thought

    B. Formal operations

    C. Concrete operations

    D. Sensorimotor

    E. Pre-operational

The answer is A.
Piaget's theory ends at the formal operations stage. Other researchers propose that an additional stage of thought occurs beyond this stage, characterized by subtleties of thinking that extend beyond formal operations. This stage is referred to as postformal thought or postformal operations.

19. **Teresa is a 31-year-old woman who is seeing a psychoanalytic therapist. The therapy sessions are currently focusing on Teresa's tendency to choose intimate male partners who possess traits that she finds similarity to those of her father. The therapist would most likely explain this tendency in terms of**

    A. Anaclitic object choice

    B. Erotogenicity

    C. Transference

    D. Counter-transference

    E. Ego cathexis

The answer is A.
In psychoanalytic theory, anaclitic object choice is an important element in the mechanism where persons develop a tendency to pursue intimate partners who resemble a parental figure in the hope these parent-substitutes will fulfill the needs of their ego-libido.

20. **In cognitive psychology, what is the term applied to the proposed mechanism of language acquisition where children are able to generate a new hypothesis based on even one single exposure to a unit of information?**

   A. Referent selection

   B. Associative proposal

   C. Whole-object bias

   D. Cross situational learning

   E. Fast mapping

The answer is E.
Fast mapping is a proposed mechanism to explain, in part, how young children are able to acquire a huge vocabulary in a relatively short period of time. The actual means that children use to accomplish this feat is uncertain and there are several alternative hypotheses to fast mapping.

21. **In James Marcia's identity status theory, which statement below represents the adolescent stage of identity foreclosure?**

   A. "I am going to be a fireman because my father was a fireman."

   B. "I believe in God, but I am going to investigate a wide range of religions to determine which feels right for me"

   C. "I don't really fit in with any of the social cliques at my high school, and that's fine with me"

   D. "I refuse to change who I am regardless of anyone else's opinion"

   E. "I sometimes wonder if I really have any identity at all"

The answer is A.
In Marcia's theory, identity foreclosure is an adolescent stage where individuals avoid an identity crisis by committing to an identity based on examples set by others. This allows them to choose an identity without reflecting on their true personal nature and preferences.

22. **Theorist Lev Vygotsky proposes that social interactions**

    A. Require higher-level cognitive functionality

    B. Occur in children only after they attain identity stability

    C. Play a fundamental role is the development of human cognition

    D. Are based on behavioral tendencies that are present at birth

    E. Interfere with objective awareness of existential threats

The answer is C.
The major theme of Vygotsky's sociocultural theory of human learning is that social interaction plays a fundamental role in the development of cognition. Vygotsky proposes that all higher cognitive functions arise from interactions between individuals.

23. **A retrospective study on residents in a Japanese fishing village showed that severe neurological damage occurred in many villagers during a specific time span. Researchers were able to use the study data to identify the agent that caused the neurological damage, an organic form of the heavy metal mercury. Study data also showed a direct, strong correlation between the level of severity of neurological damage in subjects of the study and the total amount of fish consumed from the bay of the village during a critical time span by subjects of the study. In this study, the level of neurological damage was the**

    A. Cohort

    B. Dependent variable

    C. Independent variable

    D. Controlled variable

    E. correlation coefficient

The answer is B.
The level of neurological damage in the study depended on the amount of fish consumed during a critical time period. The level of neurological damage is therefore the dependent variable.

24. A researcher conducted a study of a population of South Pacific Islanders and concluded, based on structured interviews, that the islanders, as a single ethnic group, had a much higher rate of acceptance of promiscuity and infidelity compared to other ethnic groups. Researchers later discovered that the islanders actually view promiscuity and infidelity at least as unfavorably as other ethnic groups, and that they, as a group, had conspired to provide the opposite impression to the original researcher as an elaborate practical joke. The erroneous conclusion in the original study represents

   A. An inadequate methodology

   B. A cultural bias of the researcher

   C. A failure to provide a control group

   D. A failure to replicate the original study before reaching a conclusion

   E. A selection bias

The answer is A.
The original investigator relied too heavily on a structured interview methodology to obtain accurate data. Additional information collected through naturalistic and structured observation could have uncovered the prevarications that occurred during the structured interviews.

25. Some females are born with condition called mosaic Turner syndrome, where some of their cells have only one X chromosome and the other cells have two X chromosomes. If 50% of a female's cells have only one X chromosome. At what stage of prenatal development did the chromosomal abnormality likely first occur?

   A. Before ovulation

   B. During ovulation

   C. After ovulation and before fertilization

   D. At the zygote stage

   E. After the zygote stage but before the fetal stage

The answer is E.
All cells with a missing chromosome will produce mitotic progeny cells with the same missing chromosome. There is only one cell at the zygote stage and earlier stages, so if the chromosome was absent at or before any of these stages, all of the cells of the body would have the same missing chromosome.

26. **The Tanner scale is used to evaluate which of the following?**

    A. External primary and secondary sex characteristics

    B. Stages of formal operations

    C. Emotional levels of maturity

    D. Levels of memory impairment

    E. Maturity levels of motor functioning

The answer is A.
The tanner scale is an assessment of external primary and secondary sex characteristics such as breast and genital size and the presence or absence of pubic hair

27. **A toddler is about to probe an electrical wall socket with a metal fork. As he moves the fork forward, he glances back at his mother and observes the mother displaying facial expression of extreme fear and disapproval. In response, the toddler withdraws the fork and looks for other forms of entertainment. The toddler during this scenario is demonstrating**

    A. Social modeling

    B. An unconditioned response

    C. Social referencing

    D. Self-preservation

    E. Mirroring

The answer is C.
Social referencing begins around the ages of 8 to 10 months in children. The term describes the assessment by the child of a caregiver's facial expressions to the child's impending actions. Negative facial expressions result in the child preempting the completion of the action.

28. **A 39-year-old woman is in her 12th week of pregnancy. Her obstetrician has recommended that she undergo chorionic villus sampling. What is the purpose of this test?**

    A. To test for chromosomal or genetic abnormalities of the fetus

    B. To determine if the fetus is at a normal developmental stage

    C. To determine if the mother has a different Rh blood type than the fetus

    D. To determine if the fetus has an adequate umbilical blood supply

    E. To test for abnormalities in the amniotic fluid surrounding the fetus.

The answer is A.
Chorionic villus sampling involves obtaining a sample of tissue from a portion of the placenta. The sample will contain fetal cell that can be analyzed for chromosomal and genetic disorders.

29. **In studies comparing the shared expression of traits between monozygotic twins raised in the same household vs. those raised in separate households, which trait should show the least environmental influence on its expression?**

    A. Eye color

    B. Male pattern baldness

    C. Adult height

    D. Intelligence

    E. Skin tone

The answer is A.
Most trait expression is influenced to some degree by environmental factors. Studies show strong environmental influence on intelligence and height. Skin tone is strongly influenced by exposure to sunlight. male-pattern baldness has a very strong genetic influence, but it occurs later in life, so any environmental influences are more likely to result in different rates of expression compared to eye color. Eye color at birth is extremely resistant to change due to environmental influences and identical twins are almost always born with the same eye color.

30. **Researchers have demonstrated that infants are capable of integrating information acquired simultaneously through at least two different senses. This ability to transfer learning from one sense to another is referred to as**

    A. Sensory indexing

    B. Synesthesia

    C. Immediate consciousness

    D. Intermodal perception

    E. Multitasking

The answer is D.
Strong evidence for intermodal perception in infants was first demonstrated in a study conducted by Melzoff and Borton in 1979. Their research showed 1-month-old infants could recognize an object based on a combination of the object's shape and the object's texture.

31. **Jennifer is a college senior. She has a few friends and a pleasant though somewhat distant relationship with her close family members. She enjoys spending time with her new boyfriend Jeff. For the first time she has someone she feels comfortable discussing very personal issues with. Jennifer now thinks she knows what qualities she is looking for in a potential husband, and she is discovering that Jeff possesses many of these qualities. Jennifer is most likely in the Erik Erikson's stage of**

    A. initiative vs. guilt

    B. industry vs. inferiority

    C. trust vs. mistrust

    D. identity vs. identity confusion

    E. Intimacy vs. isolation

The answer is E.
Persons in Erikson's intimacy vs. isolation stage of psychosocial development are resolving identity vs. role confusion and are becoming capable of forming intimate reciprocal relationships

32. **Brian is a 50-year-old man who was recently demoted by his work supervisor to a position of significantly lesser authority and monetary compensation. Brian adopts an attitude of "well, things could be worse, I'll get by." According to Hopson's model of transitions, Brian is engaging in**

    A. Role blurring

    B. Minimization

    C. Internalization

    D. Derealization

    E. Optimization

The answer is B.
In a negative role transition, there is often a reaction phase where the seriousness of the transition's personal impact is partially denied. This minimization phase can allow a person to deal with a transition that may be otherwise overwhelming.

33. **According to the principles of Social Learning Theory, vicarious reinforcement is occurring in which of the following situations?**

    A. A baseball pitcher learns to throw a curveball by watching other pitchers throw curveballs

    B. An actor visualizes an Oscar nomination resulting from successfully reproducing subtle attributes he imagines for a character he is portraying in a film

    C. A student overcomes fear of public speaking by speaking first in front of friends, than to gradually less familiar audiences

    D. A singer increases her vocal range by receiving praise from her voice coach each time she is able to reproduce a note with a pitch slightly outside of her previous range.

    E. A Basketball player modifies his ball-handling style based on spectator reactions to other player's ball-handling styles

The answer is E.
Vicarious reinforcement, as described in social learning theory, occurs by observation of both a behavior and the consequences of the behavior. In this case, the vicarious reinforcement is the positive or negative spectator reactions to particular elements of other player's ball- handling skills.

34. **Erin is a 25-year-old woman who is changing a flat tire for the first time. She is in an extremely hazardous location and must move her vehicle at least one mile uphill to remove herself from this life-threatening situation. The tire has four lug nuts. As Erin mounts a replacement tire, the four lug nuts fall down a steep embankment and are irretrievable. Erin devises a temporary solution for her dilemma by removing one lug nut from each of the other three tires and using the three lug nuts to satisfactorily mount the replacement tire. According to Robert Sternberg's theory, Erin's thought process demonstrates**

   A. Risk and resilience

   B. Pragmatism

   C. Prosocial behavior

   D. Role transitioning

   E. High Intelligence

The answer is E.
By any definition, Erin is demonstrating high intelligence. Sternberg's theory postulates three general categories of intelligence: 1) **Analytical intelligence** refers to problem-solving abilities. 2) **Creative intelligence** involves the ability to deal with new situations based on past experiences and current skills. 3) **Practical intelligence** involves the ability to adapt to a changing environment. Erin's solution demonstrates exceptional performance as defined for all three forms of intelligence.

35. **Which of the following is an example of an occurrence of semantic under extension?**

   A. A child refers to all four-legged creatures as "cats"

   B. A child refers to the family cats as cats but does not refer to other cats as cats

   C. A child refers to a gardener as a "plant-man."

   D. A child assumes the family dog, named Fido, is a "Fido" and refers to all other dogs are "Fidos."

   E. A child states: "I home," meaning "I am at home."

The answer is B.
Semantic underextension occurs when a word is used with a narrower meaning than it has in adult speech. In example B, a cat is only a cat if it is a family cat.

36. **In terms of age-normal visual ability, an 8-month-old infant**

    A. Cannot focus on objects between eight and 15 inches away

    B. Cannot focus on objects greater than 3 feet away

    C. Cannot discriminate between basic colors

    D. Has limited depth perception

    E. Has normal adult vision

The answer is D.
Depth perception in infants begins to develop between four and seven months, but will not reach normal adult acuity until the child is two years of age or older.

37. **B.F. Skinner's theory of language acquisition proposes that**

    A. Language acquisition occurs by reinforcement.

    B. Children are born with an innate universal grammar ability

    C. Children have an highly refined ability to recognize patterns in language

    D. Children are born with an ability to recognize any phoneme in any language

    E. Acquisition of language occurs by a gradual pattern learning process based on the concept of "morphemes."

The answer is A.
Skinner's theory is a behaviorist theory. It proposes that when a child uses verbal language correctly and subsequently receives a smile or other rewarding response from a caregiver, this correct usage of language is positively reinforced. This process continues with reinforcement of increasingly difficult language usage until fluency is achieved.

38. **An 8-year-old boy has been classified as having a moderate intellectual disability. Based on this classification, which of the following statements is true regarding the child?**

    A. He can learn up to a normal sixth grade level

    B. He has poor social awareness

    C. He has poor motor coordination

    D. He has an IQ between 70 and 90

    E. He has extremely limited cognition

The answer is B.
Children with a diagnosis of moderate intellectual disability can learn communication but have poor social awareness. Their IQ is in the 36 to 51 range.

39. **Research has shown that older people tend to have lower IQ scores than younger people. The Flynn effect states that this age related difference in IQ scores is**

    A. Evidence that intelligence decreases with age

    B. Due to a worldwide increase in IQ scores at a rate of 3 points per decade

    C. A consequence of lower motivation to test well in older persons rather than an actual lower average IQ in older persons

    D. A result of a strong correlation between increasing IQ and mortality in World War II.

    E. A statistical failure to renormalize IQ scoring resulting in an IQ score of 110 today being equivalent to an IQ score of 100 in 1940.

The answer is B.
Numerous studies have confirmed the Flynn effect. Despite intense research there is still no convincing explanation for this robust trend of an average 3 point per decade increase in IQ scores.

40. **Each of the choices below describes a reaction by a young child to the presence of a stranger. Choose the reaction that indicates the highest level of anxiety in the child.**

    A. Running to a caregiver

    B. grabbing the caregiver's legs

    C. Silence and wariness combined with a fearful facial expression

    D. Demanding to be picked up by a caregiver

    E. Refusing to look into the eyes of a stranger

The answer is C.
Choices A, B and D are typical stranger anxiety reactions in children. Choice E does not necessarily indicate anxiety. Choice C is a display of stranger terror, the most extreme form of stranger anxiety. Less extreme forms of stranger anxiety are considered normal. Stranger terror inhibits the normal functioning of the child and is an indication for a professional evaluation.

41. **In Kohlberg's theory of Cognitive development, modeling the behavior of members of the same sex occurs**

    A. After the realization that the gender of a person does not change

    B. Before the age of three

    C. Only after a child has developed the mental construct of a gender association schema

    D. With a delayed onset in single parent households where the parent is of the opposite sex

    E. As early as the first month of life

The answer is A.
Kohlberg's theory proposes that children first assign themselves a sex at approximately age 3, but do not realize that the sex of a person is permanent. Gender role reversal play is common at this stage. Around the age of 7 years, children realize through social observation and interaction that gender does not change throughout life. At this point they begin to model the behavior of members of the same sex.

42. **Choose the correct order when infants begin to demonstrate the following motor skills from the earliest to the latest age:**

    I.   **Rolls from back to side**
    II. **Holds head up when sitting**
    III. **Bears weight on forearms**

    A. I, II, III

    B. III, I, II

    C. II, III, I

    D. I, III, II

    E. III, II, I

The answer is B.
In infants, bearing weight on forearms usually begins in the third month, rolling from side to side in the fourth month, and holding head up when sitting in the fifth month.

43. **In Pavlov's experiments, dogs learned to salivate in response to an auditory cue. In later experiments these dogs began to salivate in response to a different but similar auditory cue. What is the term for this type of new response?**

    A. Operant conditioning

    B. Unconditioned

    C. Discrimination

    D. Sensitization

    E. Generalization

The answer is E.
In classical conditioning, subjects that have developed a conditioned response to a particular form of stimulation can begin to show the same conditioned response to similar stimuli. This phenomenon is termed "generalization." In this case the conditioned response is salivation.

44. **Research has shown children are more likely to have higher IQs on average if they are**

    A. An only child

    B. Female and have an older brother

    C. The second born of three siblings

    D. The second born and have no other siblings

    E. Male and have an at least one older brother

The answer is A.
A large, well-conducted study of high school students has shown that only children (children with no siblings) had better IQs on average compared to children with one or more siblings. Most other research studies suggest that IQ scores and academic performance decreases in children as their birth order and number of siblings increases.

45. **In psychology, what is a general principle that is shared by stage theory and non-stage models of information processing in humans?**

    A. Multiple neuro-anatomical locations of information storage

    B. Two-way flow of information

    C. Serial, discontinuous information processing

    D. Different levels of elaboration during information processing

    E. Lack of a biological predisposition to process information

The answer is C.
All psychological theories of information processing are in agreement that we construct meanings and relationships through dynamic processes involving the two-way flow of information which is gather through the senses and information which is stored in memory.

46. **Among the choices below, which is the recommended method of discouraging undesirable behavior in children based on the principles of operant conditioning?**

    A. Distracting the child while the behavior is occurring

    B. Punishing the behavior on a frequent but unpredictable schedule

    C. Punishing the behavior every time it occurs

    D. Rewarding the child for not engaging in the behavior for a specified period of time

    E. Rewarding the child every time the behavior is voluntarily terminated upon request

The answer is C.
Operant conditioning principles that utilize reinforcement schedules (reward and punishment) indicate that the most effective means to diminish the occurrence of an undesirable behavior is to punish every episode of such behavior. If an episode of undesirable behavior is not punished, the conditioning process must begin again. Distraction is not a principle of operant conditioning.

47. **Which type of theory proposes that a person can learn to start a fire using only naturally occurring forest resources without first practicing any of the techniques required to achieve this task?**

    A. Social cognitive

    B. Sociocultural

    C. Psychodynamic

    D. Evolutionary

    E. Behavioral

The answer is A.
Social cognitive theory asserts that learning can occur solely through a process of observation. If the individual carefully watches an expert perform a task for a sufficient amount of time, the individual may be able to replicate the task on the first attempt.

48. **A 3-year-old child has been scratched by several different cats. After investigating the family cat's paws, he discovers they contain sharp claws. The child concludes all cats can probably scratch him. What cognitive ability did the child use to reach this conclusion?**

    A. Deductive reasoning

    B. Inductive reasoning

    C. Abductive reasoning

    D. Conjectural reasoning

    E. Suppositional reasoning

The answer is B.

The process of Inductive reasoning derives general conclusions based on specific observations and/or experimentation.

49. **According to John Holland's theory, which personality type prefers physical jobs that involve skill strength and coordination?**

    A. Enterprising

    B. Social

    C. Realistic

    D. Conventional

    E. Artistic

The answer is C.

The realistic personality type in Holland's personality-type theory matches the characteristic job preference indicated in the question. Realistic personality types are also referred to as "Do-ers".They have traits considered to be stable, conforming and practical. Typical jobs preferred by realistic personality types include farmer, carpenter, truck driver and firefighter.

50. **What field of knowledge addresses the ambiguity in the statement "I saw the room with a telescope?"**

    A. Etymology

    B. Symbolics

    C. Semantics

    D. Pragmatics

    E. Lexicology

The answer is D.
Pragmatics is the linguistic subfield that addresses the meaning of language based on context. Ambiguity can arise when there is no context for a statement. By itself, the statement in the question could mean the speaker used a telescope to observe the room, or the speaker observed a room that contained a telescope. Without considering the statement within the context of a broader description, the ambiguity cannot be resolved.

51. **Severe, progressive memory loss is most characteristic of which of the following conditions?**

    A. Down's syndrome (trisomy 13)

    B. Autism

    C. Parkinson's disease

    D. Lou Gehrig's disease (ALS)

    E. Alzheimer's disease

The answer is E.
Alzheimer's disease is the most common neurological disease of the elderly. One of the most debilitating aspects of the disease is a relentless progression to near total loss of memory. Memory loss is not a significant feature of any of the other four conditions.

52. According to Elisabeth Kübler-Ross' theory, adults who erroneously believe that they could have taken actions to directly prevent the recent death of a loved one are in which stage of grief?

   A. Retrospective

   B. Denial

   C. Imaginary

   D. Bargaining

   E. Depression

The answer is D.
In Kübler-Ross' theory, the bargaining stage in grief over death is often characterized by "what if" and "if only I had" thoughts. The bargaining here represents an offer to go back in time and behave differently in exchange for avoidance of a tragic outcome.

53. What is one of the major criticisms of Piaget's principles in his theory of learning?

   A. Very young children are markedly involved in egocentric speech

   B. Research studies have shown that children can learn particular concepts before they reach prerequisite stages

   C. Other cultures have a high regard for scientific thinking

   D. Children can understand the conservation of weight and the conservation of number at the same operational stage

   E. On average, boys are able to learn particular concepts at a younger age than girls

The answer is B.
Evidence that children can learn particular concepts before the reach certain prerequisite stages contradicts a central element of Piaget's theory, namely that there are sharply defined stages that must be attained before a student will be able to learn a particular type of concept

54. **Which theorist describes the concept of the "zone of proximal development"?**

   A. Erik Erikson

   B. Jean Piaget

   C. John Holland

   D. Lev Vygotsky

   E. Robert Sternberg

The answer is D.
A key feature of Vygotsky's theory of cognitive development is the concept of the zone of proximal development (ZPD). There are two levels of attainment for the zone, the first describes what a child is capable of doing without help from others and the second describes what a child could potentially be capable with the help of more knowledgeable people, such as teachers.

55. **In behaviorist theory, habituation is occurring in which of the following scenarios?**

   A. A wife experiences increasingly strong desires for alcohol intake each succeeding night that her husband arrives home late from work

   B. Over a several month period, a child takes less time to finish a particular chore in response to his mother's constant nagging.

   C. Over time a man is able to fall asleep more easily despite the continuous nightly barking of a neighbor's dog just outside the man's bedroom window

   D. When an attractive girl smiles at a boy every time he rubs his nose, over time the boy begins to rub his nose each time the girl smiles at him

   E. A drug addict experiences increased cravings for a drug even though he is increasing the frequency that he uses the drug.

The answer is C.
In behaviorist theory, habituation is defined as a decrease in response to a stimulus after repeated presentations. In choice C, the man's response or awareness of the stimulus of the dog's barking is decreasing with each night's exposure to the barking

56. **In terms of age, from earliest to latest, in what order do children typically acquire the grammatical morphemes?**

     I.   **Regular plural – s (dog – dogs)**
    II.   **Possessive – s (Mom – Mom's)**
  III.   **Present progressive – ing (walk – walking)**

  A. I, II, III

  B. II, I, III

  C. III, II, I

  D. I, III, II

  E. III, I, II

The answer is E.
There are 14 grammatical morphemes. The first morpheme that children acquire is the present progressive – ing (walk – walking). The regular plural –s (dog - dogs) is the 4th in order of acquisition and the possessive – s (Mom – Mom's) is the 6th in order of acquisition. The contractible auxiliary (Daddy is – Daddy's) is the 14th and last acquired morpheme.

57. **Robert Sternberg's triangle theory describes three components of**

  A. Language acquisition

  B. Moral development

  C. Adult love

  D. Faith development

  E. Object relations

The answer is C.
Sternberg's triangle theory describes three components of adult love; intimacy, commitment, and passion.

58. **Stavros is a United States born, 35-year-old son of ethnic Greek immigrant parents. He is successful and happily married. He began to identify himself as ethnically Greek in his early teenage years. Today his ethnic heritage is a source of pride and this ethnic image of himself plays a major role in most aspects of his life. According to social theory, Stavros' ethnic identity …**

    A. May have replaced an earlier negative ethnic self-image

    B. Probably includes an exaggerated sense of importance of Greek culture within the overall culture of the United States

    C. Represents an internalization of his ethnicity

    D. Probably serves to mask significant insecurity issues related to his ethnic minority status

    E. Is very likely to play a diminishing role in his choice of social activities as he gets older

The answer is A.
Social theorists have observed that that ethnic identity development often begins or passes through an ethnic identity search phase, where one's ethnic identity can be a source of embarrassment and anger, frequently related to negative stereotypes and probability of low economic status of one's ethnic parents. In the ethnic identity achievement phase, the negative aspects of one's ethnic identity can be replaced by a positive, realistic, secure and stable self-image.

59. **In what age range is the initial diagnosis of schizophrenia most common?**

    A. Between 10 and 24 years

    B. Between 16 and 30 years

    C. Between 25 and 40 years

    D. Between 45 and 59 years

    E. After age 60 years

The answer is B.
The age at initial schizophrenia diagnosis for men is most common between 16 and 25 years with an average age at diagnosis at age 18. Women tend to develop the disease several years later than men, with an average age at diagnosis of 25 years.

60. A research study follows 100 children with a history of lead exposure for a 10-year period. They each are administered three separate standardized tests each year. The results are compared to score distribution curves for the tests results of all children of the same age nationwide who took the tests in the same years. What is the cohort in this study?

   A. Lead exposure

   B. The group of 100 children

   C. The three standardized tests

   D. The 10-year period

   E. The nationwide test score distribution curves

The answer is B.
The study described above is a cohort study. In cohort studies a group of subjects, often with a common risk factor, are followed over time and data is collected about the group. The subject group is called the cohort. In this case, the cohort is the group of 100 children with a history of lead exposure.

61. A young child who is using telegraphic speech is

   A. Using one word to function as a full sentence

   B. Compressing a grammatically correct statement into a two-word statement lacking conjunctions or articles

   C. Speaking with an exaggerated tone and rhythm

   D. Speaking softly in a manner not directed at or intended for others to hear

   E. Verbally conveying a thought that is intelligible and grammatically correct

The answer is B.
Telegraphic speech is an efficient form of speech that uses a two or three word phrase to convey the meaning of a more complex phrase, such As "Mommy sad" in place of "mommy is sad."

62. **Which researcher's work has shown that newborns younger than 8 months appear to have an innate ability to universally distinguish all fundamentally unique speech sounds, and that this ability is not present in adults who are learning a new language?**

   A. Noam Chomsky

   B. Anne Fernald

   C. Jenny Saffran

   D. Richard Montague

   E. Janet Werker

The answer is E.
Janet Werker's research showed that language acquisition begins with learning to recognize language -specific speech sounds called phonemes. Infants younger than 8 months can perceive phonemes in any language, but this ability is completely lost by 11 to 13 months of age.

63. **According to Lawrence Kolberg's theory, a teenage that arrives at a moral judgment of an act by considering the social consequences of the act is in what stage of moral development?**

   A. Pre-conventional

   B. conventional

   C. post-conventional

   D. empirical

   E. transcendental

The answer is B.
In Kohlberg's stages of moral development, individuals who evaluate the morality of an action based on a comparison with society's views and expectations of the action are in the conventional stage.

64. **Researchers using data collected from a study find there is a linear relationship between two variables. If the correlation coefficient (r) is calculated from a graph plot of the data, which of the correlation coefficient values shown below would indicate the strongest relationship between the two variables?**

   A. 0.2

   B. -0.9

   C. 0.5

   D. -0.1

   E. 0.0

The answer is B.
The Pearson correlation coefficient (r), is a measure of the strength and direction of a linear relationship. A perfect correlation between two variables is r=1 for a direct relationship and -1 for an inverse relationship. The strongest correlation in the answer is choices is -0.9, which indicates a very strong inverse relationship between the two variables.

65. **Mildred Parten's theory and classification of play participation in children describes activities that are interactive but lacking in formal rules or organization as**

   A. Parallel play

   B. Independent play

   C. Associative play

   D. Immature play

   E. Chaotic play

The answer is C.
Associative play involves interaction with other players, compared to the non-interactivity of the preceding stage of parallel play but a lacking in formal rules or synchronization of activity seen in the succeeding stage of cooperative play.

66. **According to psychological theories of cognitive development, which of the following tasks requires the highest level of executive function?**

    A. Selecting the most qualified persons to fill management positions in a company

    B. Accurately predicting trends in emerging markets

    C. Developing strong interpersonal relationships with important business clients

    D. Providing persuasive testimony in support of desirable regulatory legislation

    E. Devising novel, focused adaptations to a complex, rapidly changing business environment

The answer is E.
Executive function abilities relate to how accurately, rapidly and flexibly people can organize, solve, or otherwise adapt to tasks in a complex environment. Self-control, focused attention and cognitive flexibility (thinking "outside the box,") are central features of executive function.

67. **What is a valid evolutionary explanation for the relative success of societies that place a high value on the contributions of their elderly citizens to the well-being of the society?**

    A. There is a very small percentage of elderly persons in such societies

    B. Insufficient time has passed for evolutionary process to have selected out these societies

    C. Such societies are geographically isolated from other societies.

    D. The elderly in these societies provide information and services that increase the likelihood that children will survive and produce viable offspring

    E. An individual's longevity is correlated with high reproductive success during the individual's fertile years.

The answer is D.
An erroneous assumption of the principles of evolution is that individuals who are past their reproductive years provide no evolutionary advantage to a population, or are in fact a disadvantage to a population. The accumulated wisdom and skills of elderly persons can provide significant survival advantages to a particular population. There is no evidence for or there is direct evidence against the other choices. Therefore they are not valid.

68. **Research has shown that the divorce rate in the United States is**

   A. Lower for couples who both have a 4-year college degree compared to those with only a high school degree

   B. Lower for second marriages compared to first marriages

   C. Lower for Black couples than Hispanic couples

   D. Lower in couples who cohabitate before marriage compared to couples who do not cohabitate before marriage

   E. Lower for couples who marry at a young age compared to couples who marry later in life

The answer is A.
As of 2013, The U.S. Bureau of labor Statistics shows that divorce rates decrease as the educational level of couples increase

69. **In infants who are exclusively breast-fed beyond the age of six months, which nutrient is not provided is sufficient amounts?**

   A. Vitamin A

   B. Protein

   C. Riboflavin

   D. Vitamin B-12

   E. Iron

The answer is E.
Breast milk does not provide adequate iron to meet a growing child's daily intake requirement. This will eventually lead to anemia and other harmful health consequences of iron deficiency. Infants younger than six months have adequate iron stores to make up for the shortfall of iron provided by an exclusively breast-fed diet.

70. **Which of the following cognitive skills does not normally decline in an individual as a result of aging?**

   A. Fluid intelligence

   B. Recall of recent events

   C. Divided attention

   D. Vocabulary

   E. Word retrieval

The answer is D.
Most cognitive skills do decline from peak ability as persons get older. Crystallized intelligence (based on knowledge or experience accumulated over time), focused attention and most verbal abilities, including vocabulary, tend to remain stable over time.

71. **Miranda is an 18-year-old woman who has an overwhelming fear of spiders. A clinical psychologist has recommended that Amanda undergo a course of aversion therapy in order to overcome this abnormal level of fear. What is the theoretical basis for this form of therapy?**

   A. Operant conditioning

   B. Classical conditioning

   C. Principles of psychoanalysis

   D. Principles of social cognition

   E. Principles of Socratic methodology

The answer is B.
In this case, aversion therapy uses the operant conditioning concept of habituation to decrease the fear response to the negative stimulus of thoughts or actual sightings of spiders by repeatedly exposing the subject to pictures of spiders or actual spiders!

72. **Ingrid is a young woman who has completed a Big Five standardized personality inventory questionnaire. She scores highly in one of the five personality dimensions indicating she strongly prefers planned behaviors over spontaneous behaviors. What personality dimension is this?**

    A. Openness to experience

    B. Conscientiousness

    C. Extraversion

    D. Agreeableness

    E. Neuroticism

The answer is C.
The conscientiousness personality dimension is also referred to as the efficient/organized vs. easy-going/careless dimension. High conscientiousness correlates with a preference for planned rather than spontaneous behavior.

73. **Deborah is a private tutor for a 5ᵗʰ grade student, Rick, who is having difficulty with the task of determining the slope of a line from a graph. Deborah's teaching method begins with choosing an interesting graphing task and then guiding Rick in a step by step fashion through the process of plotting data on a graph and then obtaining the slope of the resulting line. Successive lessons involve less input by Deborah until Rick is able to determine the slope of a line without Deborah's assistance. What is the term for this learning process?**

    A. Cognitive guidance

    B. Instructional scaffolding

    C. Semiotic instruction

    D. Pedagogy

    E. Inquiry learning

The answer is B.
Instructional scaffolding is a teaching method that involves tailoring instruction to provide an interesting task, then providing sufficient instructor support to achieve the task. Support is gradually withdrawn as the student becomes more proficient at solving similar tasks.

74. **Peyton is a 17-year-old girl who has never had a menstrual period. A physical examination the previous year showed no physical abnormalities. Among the choices below what is an important possible explanation for Peyton's delayed menarche?**

    A. Undiagnosed herpes simplex infection

    B. Excessive dietary iron intake

    C. Food allergies

    D. Pregnancy

    E. Lack of physical exercise

The answer is D.
It is important for women to realize that they can become pregnant during their first ovulatory cycle and that the pregnancy will suppress further ovulatory cycles. Delayed menarche may be due to an unsuspected pregnancy.

75. **Bevan is a 15-year-old boy who emigrated to the United States with his biological parents 12 years ago. Bevan has maintained a 4.0 grade point average throughout his elementary and high school career. His teachers all agree that Bevan has always been exceptionally motivated to perform well in school. Among the choices below, which is most likely to account for Bevan's high motivation to achieve academic success?**

    A. Both parents have high IQs

    B. A higher socioeconomic status compared to most other student's households.

    C. High resiliency due to exposure to significant but manageable environmental stress at a young age.

    D. A compensatory response to perceived ethno-cultural prejudice

    E. A cultural background that emphasizes the importance of academic achievement

The answer is E.
Environmental factors that affect early cognitive development include differences in the level of emphasis or importance that a culture assigns to formal education. The level of motivation to perform well in school is strongly correlated to the degree of importance an individual's culture assigns to academic performance.

76. **Vertigo that is not caused by an abnormality occurring inside the brain is most likely to be caused by**

    A. Abnormal functioning of the semicircular canals

    B. Damage to the retina

    C. Abnormal hormone levels

    D. Damage to a large peripheral motor nerve

    E. Small nerve damage in patients with diabetes

The answer is A.
Vertigo is an abnormal sensation of spinning or dizziness. When it is not due to a process occurring in the brain the most likely source is the semicircular canals. They are located in the inner ear and detect changes in motion of the head. Injury or disease affecting their function typically causes vertigo.

77. **Paul, a 10-year-old boy, has observed that another student at school, Tim, is the object of ridicule by a clique of peers that Paul considers to be "the cool kids". Paul decides to punch Tim in the face. If Paul's decision was motivated by the fact that the "in crowd "clique was sure to witness his assault on Tim, Paul's behavior is most likely an example of**

    A. Passive-aggressive behavior

    B. Instrumental aggression

    C. Scapegoating

    D. Dehumanization

    E. Subservience

The answer is B.
Psychologists classify instrumental aggression as aggression perpetrated by an attacker for the purpose of attaining a reward. In this case, Paul anticipates improved esteem and social position among a desired social group as a reward for his attack on Tim.

78. **A young boy observes that his father always mows the lawn and that his mother always does the laundry. From these observations and others in the outside world he has concluded that men are physically strong and women are comparatively physically weak. Over time the boy develops a mental catalogue of this and other gender related connections. In gender schema theory, this mental framework**

   A. Is required to allow the boy to assign himself a gender

   B. Leads to the recognition that gender is constant throughout life

   C. Provides a mechanism to evaluate discrepancies observed in gender based behavior in other individuals

   D. Influences judgments about behavior and promotes gender stereotyping

   E. Is an example of generalized behavior pattern seen in most mammals that live in herds or other extended groups

The answer is D.
In Schema theory, the mental framework that organizes gender relevant information tends to identify discrepancies in gender behavior, such as a father changing a baby's diaper, as a mismatch, or inappropriate behavior. This can lead to gender stereotyping.

79. **What theorist proposed an explanation of personality based on conscious forces and unconscious desires and beliefs?**

   A. Sigmund Freud

   B. Jean Piaget

   C. Hans Jürgen Eysenck

   D. Raymond Cattell

   E. Urie Bronfenbrenner

The answer is A.
Freud's theory proposes that personality develops from an interplay of conscious information at a given time such as sights, sounds, hunger, and emotions; preconscious information, such as basic information stored in memories that is immediately retrievable, and unconscious thoughts, feelings and desires whose influence on our lives is always present, but of which we are unaware.

80. **Beginning around the age of three to four months, what is most likely to elicit laughter from a child?**

    A. Actions that involve another child close to their own age

    B. Interactions with a household pet

    C. Interactions with caregivers that deviate from normal interactions

    D. Actions that result in laughter from a caregiver

    E. Interactions that occur in a group activity of three or more persons including the child

The answer is C.
Laughter in infants around the age of three to four months is an indication that they are able to recognize incongruities. Typically laughter is elicited by events and actions that represent deviations from what was expected.

81. **Akihiro's native language is Japanese. He is twenty-five years old and began learning English five years ago. He has achieved professional working fluency in English, but tests conducted by a linguistic audiologist confirms he is unable to detect the difference between the English "L" and "R" sounds. For example, the words "lent" and "rent" sound the same to him. This is an example of**

    A. Aphonia

    B. Echolalia

    C. Categorical perception

    D. Dyslexia

    E. Atonic dissonance

The answer is C.
Categorical perception in speech occurs when the difference between two or more different sounds are processed by the brain as being close enough to fall into the category of a single sound. This is important because no two individual speakers produce exactly the same sounds when they speak the same words. In Japanese speech, there is insufficient distinction between the English "l" and "r" sounds to identify them as separate speech sounds. Native Japanese speakers can hear no difference between the two sounds.

82. **Sarah is an 8-year-old girl who was born with a group of characteristic abnormal facial features. Her development of many gross and fine motor skills occurred at a significantly later age than normal. She suffers from mental retardation, impaired language development and seizures. During Sarah's prenatal development, which of the factors described below is the most likely explanation for her condition?**

     A. Inadequate thiamine intake by the mother

     B. Heavy alcohol use by the mother

     C. Heavy marijuana use by the mother

     D. Undiagnosed diabetes in the mother

     E. Heavy cigarette smoking by the mother

The answer is B.
All of the choices are risk factors to the health and development of children during perinatal development. Among the choices, only heavy alcohol use is associated with the constellation of signs and symptoms described for Sarah. The condition is called fetal alcohol syndrome (FAS) and is one of the most common causes of preventable mental retardation. Between 5,000 and 12,000 children are born with FAS in the U.S. each year. (Tag: biological development; multiple subcategories.)

83. **Margaret is a 40-year-old independent consultant who was recently hired by a large company because of Margaret's track record of utilizing multiple highly effective strategies to provide solutions to companies who were experiencing serious, complex and unexpected problems. Margaret's value to her clients, in psychological terms, is her**

     A. Altruism

     B. Pragmatism

     C. Wisdom

     D. Expertise

     E. Resilience

The answer is D.
Expertise in psychology refers to the group of qualities that distinguish an expert from a novice. The description of Margaret's marketable qualities are considered to be the most important set of distinctions between expert and novice task performance and problem solving.

84. **In Psychology, risk and resiliency theories would most likely propose a mechanism to explain which of the following observations?**

    A. In a controlled situation, a driver demonstrates lower than expected impairment of driving skills while under the influence of alcohol

    B. Some employees are able to perform tasks exceptionally well in a rapidly changing work environment

    C. Teenagers sharing certain types of interpersonal relationships are less likely to engage in drug use

    D. An undesirable behavior continues to recur despite repeated application of negative reinforcement schedules

    E. A religious practice among a group persists despite decades of repression by a government

The answer is C.
Risk and resilience theories in psychology propose mechanisms to explain why some individuals or groups of individuals are more resistant to social and environmental risk factors than others who are exposed to the same types and levels of risks.

85. **A 50-year-old woman has end-stage pancreatic cancer. Her physicians have recommended her transfer to a facility that will provide care and treatment that provide comfort but no further treatment that is designed to alter the course of her disease. In the United States, what is the term for this type of care?**

    A. Custodial

    B. Minimal

    C. Euthanasia

    D. Supportive

    E. Hospice

The answer is E.
Hospice care facilities in the U.S. are reserved for patients with a terminal diagnosis and who usually have less than six months to live. Treatment is provided to make the patients as comfortable as possible, but all medical attempts to alter the course of the terminal condition are withheld. (Tag: family home and society; subcategory: death and dying)

86. In substance abuse and compulsive behavior intervention programs, which of the following encourage the subject of the intervention to adopt a set of guiding principles?

    A. Twelve-step programs

    B. Paradoxical intervention programs

    C. Primal therapy programs

    D. Transference interpretation programs

    E. Behavioral therapy intervention programs

The answer is A.
12-step programs historically are based on the original program proposed for alcohol addiction by Alcoholics Anonymous. There are variations in the specifics of the guiding principles among the various programs, but all 12-step programs are based on this concept.

87. Critics of evolutionary theories of social behavior claim certain prosocial behaviors cannot be explained based on the principles of evolution. Which of the following is an example of this type of prosocial behavior?

    A. Altruism

    B. Nepotism

    C. Cooperativism

    D. Commensalism

    E. hedonism

The answer is A.
Prosocial behavior is a broad range of behaviors that are characterized by a concern for the rights, feelings and welfare of others. Altruism is an extreme form of prosocial behavior where there is arguably either no identifiable survival advantage or even a negative survival advantage conveyed to persons who engage in the behavior.

88. **Jerry is a 30-year-old man who is interviewing for a job. During the interview, Jerry engages in subconscious behavior to build rapport with the interviewer. Jerry is most likely**

    A. Misdirecting

    B. Patronizing

    C. Mirroring

    D. Supplicating

    E. Soliciting

The answer is C.
Mirroring is an often unconscious or covert imitation of another person's facial expressions and physical gestures. The behavior is first seen in infants and is a mechanism designed to make a positive social connection.

89. **Douglas is a 26-year-old man who is widely regarded by his family and friends as a person with a very optimistic attitude. Whenever Doug experiences a negative event in his life he is more likely to attribute the cause of the event to**

    A. Random chance instead of a specific cause

    B. An error on his part instead of someone else's

    C. A spiritual rather than a naturalistic cause

    D. A temporary set of external circumstances rather than a permanent external condition

    E. Unavoidable external rather than avoidable external circumstances

The answer is D.
The attributional explanatory style associated with optimistic personalities views the causes of negative events as being temporary rather than permanent, external rather than one's own fault, and due to specific rather than global circumstances.

90. **Martin is a normal, healthy 5-year-old boy who has always been in the 60th percentile of height and weight for boys his age. Assuming Martin has a typical childhood environment and upbringing, with no significant health or psychiatric issues, what would be his least likely height vs. weight percentiles at age 18?**

A. 60th percentile for height vs. 60th percentile for weight

B. 60th percentile for height vs. 50th percentile for weight

C. 70th percentile for height vs. 70th percentile for weight

D. 70th percentile for height vs. 50th percentile for weight

E. 80th percentile for height vs. 70th percentile for weight.

The answer is D.
During puberty it is not uncommon for children to cross height and weight percentiles. The normal trend is that they maintain their height vs. weight percentile difference. Martin has no difference between his height and weight percentiles at age 5. The largest change in the choices above for Martin is a 20 percentile difference in choice D

Description of the Examination

The Introductory Psychology examination covers material that is usually taught in a one-semester undergraduate course in introductory psychology. It stresses basic facts, concepts and generally accepted principles in thirteen areas listed in the following section.

The examination contains approximately 95 questions to be answered in 90 minutes. Some of these are pretest questions that will not be scored. Any time candidates spend on tutorials and providing personal information is in addition to the actual testing time.

Please note that the questions on the CLEP Introductory Psychology exam will continue to adhere to the terminology, criteria and classifications referred to in the fourth edition of the *Diagnostic and Statistical Manual of Mental Disorders* (DSM-IV-TR) until further notice.

Knowledge and Skills Required

Questions on the Introductory Psychology examination require candidates to demonstrate one or more of the following abilities.

- Knowledge of terminology, principles and theory
- Ability to comprehend, evaluate and analyze problem situations
- Ability to apply knowledge to new situations

The subject matter of the Introductory Psychology examination is drawn from the following topics. The percentages next to the main topics indicate the approximate percentage of exam questions on that topic.

8%-9%   History, Approaches, Methods
- History of psychology
- Approaches: biological, behavioral, cognitive, humanistic, psychodynamic
- Research methods: experimental, clinical, correlations
- Ethics in research

8%-9%   Biological Bases of Behavior
- Endocrine system
- Etiology
- Functional organization of the nervous system
- Genetics
- Neuroanatomy
- Physiological techniques

7%-8%   Sensation and Perception
- Attention
- Other senses: somesthesis, olfaction, gustation, vestibular system
- Perceptual development
- Perceptual process
- Receptor processes: vision, audition
- Sensory mechanisms: thresholds, adaptation

5%-6%   States of Consciousness
- Hypnosis and meditation
- Psychoactive drug effects
- Sleep and dreaming

10%-11%   Learning
- Biological bases
- Classical conditioning
- Cognitive process in learning
- Observational learning
- Operant conditioning

8%-9% **Cognition**
- Intelligence and creativity
- Language
- Memory
- Thinking and problem solving

7%-8% **Motivation and Emotion**
- Biological bases
- Hunger, thirst, sex, pain
- Social motivation
- Theories of emotion
- Theories of motivation

8%-9% **Developmental Psychology**
- Dimensions of development: physical, cognitive, social, moral
- Gender identity and sex roles
- Heredity-environment issues
- Research methods: longitudinal, cross-sectional
- Theories of development

7%-8% **Personality**
- Assessment techniques
- Growth and adjustment
- Personality theories and approaches
- Research methods: idiographic, nomothetic
- Self-concept, self-esteem

8%-9% **Psychological Disorders and Health**
- Affective disorders
- Anxiety disorders
- Dissociative disorders
- Health, stress and coping

- Personality disorders
- Psychoses
- Somatoform disorders
- Theories of psychopathology

7%-8% **Treatment of Psychological Disorders**
- Behavioral therapies
- Biological and drug therapies
- Cognitive therapies
- Community and preventive approaches
- Insight therapies: psychodynamic and humanistic approaches

7%-8% **Social Psychology**
- Aggression/antisocial behavior
- Attitudes and attitude change
- Attribution processes
- Conformity, compliance, obedience
- Group dynamics
- Interpersonal perception

3%-4% **Statistics, Tests and Measurement**
- Descriptive statistics
- Inferential statistics
- Measurement of intelligence
- Mental handicapping conditions
- Reliability and validity
- Samples, populations, norms
- Types of tests

SAMPLE TEST

DIRECTIONS: Read each item and select the best response.

1. **Which of the following describes an expression of favor or disfavor for a person, place, thing, or event?**

   A. Attitude

   B. Belief

   C. Cognition

   D. Drive

   E. Behavior

2. **Which of the following is a theory by Ajzen and Fishbein that outlines a model for the prediction of behavioral intention?**

   A. Cognitive Dissonance Theory

   B. Social Judgment Theory

   C. Theory of Reasoned Action

   D. Information Integration Theory

   E. Congruity Theory

3. **According to Petty and Cacioppo's Elaboration Likelihood Model, when a person is persuaded by the likeability of a speaker, he or she is using which processing route?**

   A. Central

   B. Heuristic

   C. Peripheral

   D. Systemic

   E. None of the above

4. **Which of the following psychologists coined the term *group dynamics* to describe the positive and negative forces within groups of people?**

   A. Maslow

   B. Lewin

   C. Freud

   D. Pavlov

   E. Skinner

5. **Which of the following "deals with how the social perceiver uses information to arrive at causal explanations for events?"**

   A. Cognitive Dissonance Theory

   B. Classical conditioning

   C. Psychoanalysis

   D. Attribution Theory

   E. Frequency Theory

6. **Which of the following describes obedience?**

   A. The act of changing one's beliefs and attitudes to match those of other members of a social group

   B. The act of following orders without question because they come from a legitimate authority

   C. The act of adapting one's actions to another's wishes or rules

   D. The act of influencing another's attitudes, beliefs, or behaviors

   E. The act of establishing credibility and authority

7. **Paul is driving to work when another driver cuts him off in traffic. Paul begins shouting and pounding on the steering wheel. Paul is exhibiting _____.**

   A. passive aggression

   B. passivity

   C. instrumental aggression

   D. dissociative rage

   E. impulsive aggression

8. **According to Maslow's Hierarchy of Needs, humans must satisfy their physiological needs before they will desire to satisfy which other category of needs?**

   A. Safety

   B. Belonging

   C. Esteem

   D. Self-actualization

   E. All of the above

9. **Which of the following is considered a prosocial emotion?**

   A. Anger

   B. Sadness

   C. Shame

   D. Happiness

   E. Awe

10. **Which of the following statements is true of long-term memory?**

    A. Long-term memory has nearly infinite storage capacity.

    B. Long-term memory is also known as working memory.

    C. Long-term memory allows people to temporarily store and manipulate visual images.

    D. Long-term memory has a shorter duration than working memory.

    E. None of the above statements are true of long-term memory.

11. **The term *chunking* refers to**

    A. transferring memories from short-term to long-term

    B. combining small bits of information into larger, familiar pieces

    C. sensory memory

    D. repeating information over and over to increase the duration of time in which it stays in short-term memory

    E. an organizational process for cataloguing memories

12. **The smallest units of speech are called**

    A. vowels

    B. syllables

    C. phonemes

    D. semantic

    E. syntax

13. **Which of the following terms describes the process by which memories fade over time?**

   A. Memory loss

   B. Memory fade

   C. Memory decay

   D. Memory delay

   E. Memory recall

14. **The study of psychology began in _____ and was established by _____.**

   A. The United States; Freud

   B. Germany; Freud

   C. Germany; Ebbinghaus

   D. The United States; Skinner

   E. France; Piaget

15. **Conduction aphasia is caused by which of the following?**

   A. Disruptions in the connection between the Wernicke's and Broca's areas

   B. Disruptions in the ability to consolidate information at a neural level

   C. Short-term memory loss due to retrograde amnesia

   D. Blockage of neural circuits in working memory

   E. Damage to the cerebellum

16. **An experiment that produces identical results each time is considered which of the following?**

   A. Valid, but not reliable

   B. Reliable, but not valid

   C. Valid and reliable

   D. Reliable with questionable validity

   E. Valid with questionable reliability

17. The assumption that maladaptive thought patterns and behaviors are learned is associated with which of the following?

   A. Behavioral therapy

   B. Cognitive therapy

   C. Psychoanalytic therapy

   D. Rogerian therapy

   E. Group therapy

18. You have conducted two experiments in which you failed to get the same result although the conditions under which both experiments are identical. It is clear that the measurement lacks which of the following?

   A. Face validity

   B. Construct validity

   C. Inter-rater reliability

   D. Reliability

   E. Internal validity

19. When is punishment most effective is changing or suppressing behavior?

   A. Punishment is most effective when it is delayed, inconsistent, and mild.

   B. Punishment is most effective when it is immediate, consistent, and intense.

   C. Punishment is most effective when it is explained.

   D. Punishment is most effective when it is immediate, consistent, and mild.

   E. Punishment is most effective when it is vague.

20. A psychologist administers the same IQ test three times to the same subject and receives identical or similar results each time. However, many scholars argue that IQ tests do not measure intelligence, but rather measure one's test-taking ability. This suggests that IQ tests are which of the following?

   A. Valid but not reliable

   B. Both valid and reliable

   C. Neither valid nor reliable

   D. Reliable but not valid

   E. Lacking internal reliability

21. **Which of the following attempts to establish an unpleasant response to the object that produces an undesired behavior?**

    A. Systematic desensitization

    B. Implosion therapy

    C. Aversive classical conditioning

    D. Punishment

    E. Unconditioned stimulus

22. **The ability to imitate the behavior of others and perform the same behavior under the same or similar conditions describes which of the following?**

    A. Modeling

    B. Shaping

    C. Imitation

    D. Reinforcement

    E. Play

23. **Which approach to psychology suggests that people are controlled by their environments?**

    A. Humanism

    B. Behaviorism

    C. Psychodynamic

    D. Cognitive

    E. Biological

24. **Which of the following statements best describes the evolutionary perspective of psychology?**

    A. The evolutionary approach explains human behavior in terms of classical and operational conditioning.

    B. The evolutionary approach studies the effects of genes on human behavior.

    C. The evolutionary approach seeks to understand the function of different mental processes.

    D. The evolutionary approach explains human behavior in terms of the selective pressures that shape behavior.

    E. The evolutionary approach seeks to study the whole person.

25. Which of the following psychologist founded the psychodynamic perspective of psychology?

    A. Sigmund Freud

    B. Ivan Pavlov

    C. B. F. Skinner

    D. Abraham Maslow

    E. Carl Rogers

26. Jane's experiment did not produce significant results and she is afraid that her paper will not get published. She decides to change some of the numbers in her data to get the outcome she desired. Jane has violated which general principle of ethics, according to the APA?

    A. Beneficence

    B. Fidelity

    C. Responsibility

    D. Justice

    E. Integrity

27. With which of the following research methods does the observer have direct contact with the group he or she is observing?

    A. Field experiment

    B. Participant observation

    C. Laboratory experiment

    D. Natural observation

    E. Controlled observation

28. The requirement that researchers explain to potential participants the purpose and nature of a study, as well as any possible risks associated with participation, is known as

    A. informed consent

    B. integrity

    C. researcher responsibility

    D. liability

    E. confidentiality

29. Which of the following topics do cognitive psychologists study?

    A. Behavior

    B. Emotion

    C. Self-actualization

    D. Memory and learning

    E. Genes and DNA

30. **Which of the following psychologists can be categorized as a humanist?**

    A. Sigmund Freud

    B. Ivan Pavlov

    C. B. F. Skinner

    D. Abraham Maslow

    E. Wilhelm Wundt

31. **Which of the following prevents a person from moving while experiencing dreams?**

    A. REM atonia

    B. NREM sleep

    C. Muscle relaxers

    D. Beta waves

    E. Alpha waves

32. **During the beginning of sleep, when a person is still relatively awake, the brain produces**

    A. Rapid Eye Movement

    B. Beta Waves

    C. Alpha waves

    D. Hallucinations

    E. None of the above

33. **Dreaming most often occurs during which phase of sleep?**

    A. Stage 1 (theta waves)

    B. Stage 2 (sleep spindles)

    C. Stage 3 (delta waves)

    D. Stage 4 (REM)

    E. Dreaming occurs in all of the above stages

34. **Which of the following is NOT considered a benefit of meditation?**

    A. Greater capacity for empathy

    B. Decreased stress

    C. Increased anxiety

    D. Increased gray matter in the brain

    E. Improved sleep

35. **Research on sleep provides evidence to support the ideas that**

    A. sleep is not necessary in the production of brain proteins

    B. all individuals require at least 8 hours of sleep each night for optimal functioning

    C. low-quality sleep and sleep deprivation negatively impact mood

    D. sleep does not impact learning

    E. sleep is not essential to well-being

36. **A dog learns that when it rings a bell, its owner will let it outside. This is an example of which kind of learning?**

    A. Modeling

    B. Classical conditioning

    C. Instrumental conditioning

    D. Stimulus control

    E. Operant conditioning

37. **Which of the following types of learning involves reinforcement and punishment?**

    A. Operant conditioning

    B. Classical conditioning

    C. Habituation

    D. Instrumental conditioning

    E. Modeling

38. **Which of the following types of learning involves a stimulus and response?**

    A. Operant conditioning

    B. Classical conditioning

    C. Habituation

    D. Instrumental conditioning

    E. Modeling

39. **Which of the following depicts Freud's stages of psychosexual development in the correct order?**

    A. Oral, phallic, anal, latent, genital

    B. Genital, phallic, anal, latent, oral

    C. Phallic, oral, anal, genital, latent

    D. Oral, anal, phallic, latent, genital

    E. Anal, oral, latent, phallic, genital

40. **According to Piaget, the sensorimotor stage occurs between which ages?**

    A. 0-2 years

    B. 2-7 years

    C. 7-11 years

    D. 11-15 years

    E. 15+ years

41. **Piaget's theory of cognitive development is concerned with which population?**

    A. Newborn babies

    B. Children of all ages

    C. Young adults

    D. Mature adults

    E. Elderly adults

42. **Which theory explains how parent-child relationships emerge and influence subsequent development?**

    A. Psychoanalytic theory

    B. Social learning theory

    C. Cognitive development

    D. Attachment theory

    E. None of the above

43. **Developmental psychologists often prefer which type of research design?**

    A. Experimental

    B. Participant observation

    C. Case study

    D. Cross-sectional

    E. Longitudinal

44. **On which level of Kohlberg's moral stages is a child whose morality is based on rules and punishments?**

    A. Level I. Pre-conventional/premoral

    B. Level II: Conventional/Role conformity

    C. Level III: Post-conventional/Self-accepted moral principles

    D. Level IV: Fully moral

    E. None of the above

45. **Which of the following disorders is characterized by hallucinations and delusions such as hearing voices?**

    A. Depression

    B. Obsessive compulsive disorder

    C. Bipolar disorder

    D. Schizophrenia

    E. Mania

46. **Which of the following drugs has stimulant and hallucinogenic effects?**

    A. Molly

    B. Adderall

    C. Marijuana

    D. Cocaine

    E. Pain killers

47. **Jimmy is experiencing recurring negative thoughts, a loss of interest in activities that used to excite him, trouble sleeping, and a loss of appetite. From which of the following disorders is Jimmy most likely suffering?**

    A. Depression

    B. Obsessive compulsive disorder

    C. Bipolar disorder

    D. Schizophrenia

    E. Mania

48. **Which of the following anxiety disorders is characterized by a fear of losing control, being trapped, or panicking in public places?**

    A. Acrophrobia

    B. Agoraphobia

    C. Generalized anxiety disorder

    D. Post-traumatic stress disorder

    E. General panic attack

49. **Antidepressants arc often associated with which of the following side effects?**

A. Insomnia

B. Dry mouth

C. An increase in suicidal thoughts

D. Decreased sexual drive and function

E. All of the above

50. **Which of the following types of disorders is characterized by real physical symptoms that cannot be fully explained by a medical condition, the effects of a drug, or another mental disorder?**

A. Personality disorders

B. Anxiety disorders

C. Somatoform disorders

D. Affective disorders

E. Dissociative disorders

51. **Which of the following personality disorders is characterized by an exaggerate sense of self-importance, a strong desire to be admired, and a lack of empathy?**

A. Borderline personality disorder

B. Histrionic personality disorder

C. Avoidant personality disorder

D. Narcissistic personality disorder

E. Antisocial personality disorder

52. **People with which of the following personality disorders often lack empathy and remorse, and exhibit aggressive, impulsive, reckless, or irresponsible behavior?**

A. Borderline personality disorder

B. Histrionic personality disorder

C. Avoidant personality disorder

D. Narcissistic personality disorder

E. Antisocial personality disorder

53. A person who experiences depressive and manic episodes may have which of the following disorders?

    A. Depression

    B. Obsessive compulsive disorder

    C. Bipolar disorder

    D. Schizophrenia

    E. Mania

54. Hypochondria is an example of which of the following types of disorders?

    A. Personality disorders

    B. Anxiety disorders

    C. Somatoform disorders

    D. Affective disorders

    E. Dissociative disorders

55. The _____ nervous system prepares the body for action, while the _____ nervous system keeps the body still.

    A. Sympathetic, parasympathetic

    B. Autonomic, sympathetic

    C. Parasympathetic, autonomic

    D. Sympathetic, autonomic

    E. Parasympathetic, sympathetic

56. Which of the following theories of emotion suggests that people experience emotions because they perceive physiological changes in their bodies?

    A. Cognitive appraisal

    B. Schachter and Singer's Two-Factor Theory

    C. Evolutionary Theory

    D. James-Lange Theory

    E. Cannon-Bard Theory

57. Which of the following terms describes a theoretical construct that is used to explain the reasons for people's actions, desires, and needs?

    A. Emotion

    B. Empathy

    C. Motivation

    D. Hunger

    E. Thirst

58. **Which of the following is an example of intrinsic motivation?**

    A. Money

    B. Receiving an award

    C. Feeling a sense of accomplishment

    D. Winning a prize

    E. A cheering crowd

59. **Which of the following drugs is commonly abused by college students because its stimulant effects can aid in studying?**

    A. Cocaine

    B. Marijuana

    C. Adderall

    D. Alcohol

    E. All of the above

60. **Which of the following theories suggests that we are motivated to take action based on our biological needs?**

    A. Drive reduction theory

    B. Arousal theory

    C. Instinct theory

    D. Maslow's Hierarchy of Needs

    E. Goal-setting theory

61. **Which of the following theories of emotion argues that one's experience of emotion depends on their physiological arousal and cognitive interpretation of that arousal?**

    A. Cognitive appraisal

    B. Schachter and Singer's Two-Factor Theory

    C. Evolutionary Theory

    D. James-Lange Theory

    E. Cannon-Bard Theory

62. **Which of the following is the correct term for vision that comes from the side of the eye?**

    A. Peripheral vision

    B. Tunnel vision

    C. Perceptive vision

    D. Sensation

    E. Detection

63. **Which of the following correctly lists Paiget's stages of cognitive development?**

    A. Sensorimotor, concrete operational, preoperational, formal operational

    B. Preoperational, formal operational, concrete operational. sensorimotor

    C. Formal operational, concrete operational, preoperational, sensorimotor

    D. Concrete operational, preoperational, sensorimotor, formal operational

    E. Sensorimotor, preoperational, concrete operational, formal operational

64. **Which of the following therapies is considered a last resort method of treating depression when all other therapies have failed?**

    A. Antidepressant medication

    B. Psychoanalytic therapy

    C. Cognitive-behavioral therapy

    D. Electroconvulsive shock therapy

    E. Group therapy

65. **Which of the following best describes a cross-sectional study?**

    A. A researcher follows the same participants over a period of time.

    B. A researcher examines different groups of people who share one or more similar characteristics.

    C. A researcher brings people into a lab and has them complete a task.

    D. A researcher observes people in their homes.

    E. A researcher surveys observes people in public.

66. **Psychology researchers use which of the following terms to describe thinking, reasoning, and solving problems?**

    A. Emotion

    B. Intuition

    C. Perception

    D. Sensation

    E. Cognition

67. **Lawrence Kohlberg is known for his research in the area of _____ development.**

    A. Cognitive

    B. Moral

    C. Personality

    D. Emotional

    E. Physical

68. **Which of the following statements about antidepressants do most psychology researchers and practitioners consider true?**

    A. Antidepressants are helpful in treating some forms of depression.

    B. For many patients, antidepressants are less helpful than individual therapy in treating depression.

    C. Antidepressants alone are not enough to successfully treat depression in many patients.

    D. All of the above

    E. None of the above

69. **Which of the following therapies helps people work through problems by interacting with one or more therapists as well as other individuals experiencing similar struggles?**

    A. Individual therapy

    B. Drug therapy

    C. Group therapy

    D. Psychoanalytic therapy

    E. Social-Emotional therapy

70. **According to Kübler-Ross, the correct order of the stages of grief are:**

    A. denial, anger, bargaining, depression, acceptance.

    B. anger, denial, depression, bargaining, acceptance.

    C. denial, depression, anger, acceptance, bargaining.

    D. depression, denial, anger, bargaining, acceptance.

    E. acceptance, denial, anger, bargaining, depression.

71. **Which of the following correctly describes the difference between depression and grief?**

    A. Grief often entails a sense of worthlessness whereas depression does not.

    B. Grief involves excessive guilt and depression does not.

    C. Grief lasts longer than major depression.

    D. Grief subsides after a period of time whereas depression often persists for extended periods of time.

    E. Grief is a clinical condition whereas depression is a normal, healthy emotion.

72. **Cara describes herself as outgoing, funny and friendly. These characteristics are part of her**

    A. self-esteem.

    B. motivation.

    C. self-concept.

    D. group identity.

    E. physique.

73. **In personality research, which of the following describes personal characteristics that are biologically determined?**

    A. Nature

    B. Environment

    C. State

    D. Trait

    E. Ego

74. **Which of the following is not a standard method used to assess personality?**

    A. Self-reports

    B. Observer-reports

    C. Test data

    D. Projective measures

    E. Laboratory study

75. The Big Five personality traits are:

A. Humor, openness, extraversion, agreeableness, neuroticism.

B. Extraversion, agreeableness, enlightenment, openness, neuroticism

C. Openness, conscientiousness, extraversion, agreeableness, neuroticism.

D. Extraversion, introversion, humor, neuroticism, openness

E. Happiness, neuroticism, shyness, openness, extraversion

76. _____ refers to the pattern of thoughts, feelings, social adjustments and behaviors consistently exhibited over time.

A. Preferences

B. Self-esteem

C. Construct

D. Personality

E. Extraversion

77. Conscientiousness refers to one's

A. tendency to be creative, curious, and open to new ideas.

B. tendency to be organized and self-disciplined.

C. tendency to experience unpleasant emotions easily.

D. tendency to be compassionate and cooperative towards others.

E. tendency to exhibit to seek stimulation in the company of others.

78. Which of the following types of psychologists believe that one's personality consists of learned patterns

A. Emotional psychologists

B. Humanists

C. Behavioral psychologists

D. Psychoanalytic theorists

E. Cognitive psychologists

79. Kim lives in Alaska and says that a 60-degree day is warm. Steve lives in Arizona and thinks 60-degree weather is cold. Their perceptions differ because of

    A. their frame of reference

    B. where they place their attention

    C. perceptual constancy

    D. their personalities

    E. their top-down processing

80. Which of the following terms explains why roads appear to converge in the distance?

    A. Light and shadow

    B. Continuing patterns

    C. Texture gradient

    D. Linear perspective

    E. None of the above

81. Anything that can be perceived with one of the five senses is considered _____ stimulus, whereas _____ stimulus refers to the specific object upon which one is focused.

    A. Attended, environmental

    B. Image, recognition

    C. Environmental, attended

    D. Neural, retinal

    E. Neural, image

82. An image on the retina of the eye is transformed into electrical signals in a process known as which of the following?

    A. Transcendence

    B. Abduction

    C. Transformation

    D. Intensification

    E. Transduction

83. **Which of the following is true of secondary reinforcers?**

    A. They are learned.

    B. They are ineffective.

    C. They are more effective than primary reinforcers.

    D. They are innate.

    E. They are natural.

84. **The analysis of information starting with features and building into a complete perception is known as which of the following?**

    A. Perceptual constancy

    B. Top-down processing

    C. Bottom-up processing

    D. Chunking

    E. Linking

85. **Which of the following allows humans to perceive the world in three dimensions?**

    A. Depth perception

    B. Sensation

    C. Disparity

    D. Convergence

    E. Accommodation

86. **Neurons are made up of which of the following?**

    A. Anterior cell, posterior cell, axon

    B. Dendrite, soma, axon

    C. Cell body, cell wall, nucleus

    D. Myelin, dendrite, cell wall

    E. None of the above

87. **Which of the following describes the main function of myelin?**

    A. Myelin forms a protective coating over nerve axons.

    B. Myelin decreases the speed with which information travels from nerve cell to nerve cell.

    C. Myelin blocks reception of acetylcholine.

    D. Myelin slows down nerve degeneration.

    E. Myelin aids in the transference of neurotransmitters.

88. Neurotransmitters are released at which part of a cell?

    A. Dendrite

    B. Axon terminal

    C. Nucleus

    D. Soma

    E. Myelin

89. Communication within a neuron is a(n) _____ process, while communication between neurons is a(n) _____ process.

    A. Chemical; mechanical

    B. Electrical; mechanical

    C. Chemical; electrical

    D. Electrical; chemical

    E. Mechanical; electrical

90. Human behavior is influenced by genetic processes as well their environments and experiences. In psychology, this is known as which of the following?

    A. Genes versus experience

    B. Heredity versus environment

    C. Climate versus science

    D. Nature versus nurture

    E. Genes versus personality

91. Which of the following is the main link between the brain and the glandular system in the human body?

    A. Hypothalamus

    B. Prefrontal cortex

    C. Central nervous system

    D. Sympathetic nervous system

    E. Parasympathetic nervous system

92. The endocrine system is responsible for which of the following functions?

    A. It pumps blood throughout the body.

    B. It brings oxygen into the body.

    C. It secretes hormones into the blood stream for communication between cells.

    D. It processes sensory information from the eyes and ears.

    E. None of the above.

93. **An EEG records which of the following?**

    A. The electrical rhythm of the heart.

    B. Electrical impulses from the brain.

    C. Hormone secretion in the bloodstream.

    D. Electrical currents in the body.

    E. The number of neurons in the brain.

94. **In Pavlov's famous experiment, the dog's salivation over food was considered which of the following?**

    A. Conditioned response

    B. Conditioned stimulus

    C. Automatic stimulus

    D. Unconditioned response

    E. Unconditioned stimulus

95. **Which of the following scientists is known for studying operant conditioning?**

    A. Pavlov

    B. Freud

    C. Maslow

    D. Piaget

    E. Skinner

INTRODUCTORY PSYCHOLOGY

ANSWER KEY

Question Number	Correct Answer	Your Answer	Question Number	Correct Answer	Your Answer	Question Number	Correct Answer	Your Answer
1	A		33	D		65	B	
2	C		34	C		66	E	
3	C		35	C		67	B	
4	B		36	E		68	D	
5	D		37	A		69	C	
6	B		38	B		70	A	
7	E		39	D		71	D	
8	E		40	A		72	C	
9	C		41	B		73	D	
10	A		42	D		74	E	
11	B		43	E		75	C	
12	C		44	A		76	D	
13	C		45	D		77	B	
14	C		46	A		78	C	
15	A		47	A		79	A	
16	D		48	B		80	D	
17	A		49	E		81	C	
18	D		50	C		82	E	
19	B		51	D		83	A	
20	D		52	E		84	C	
21	C		53	C		85	A	
22	A		54	C		86	B	
23	B		55	A		87	A	
24	D		56	D		88	B	
25	A		57	C		89	D	
26	E		58	C		90	D	
27	B		59	C		91	A	
28	A		60	A		92	C	
29	D		61	B		93	B	
30	D		62	A		94	D	
31	A		63	E		95	E	
32	B		64	D				

RATIONALES

1. **Which of the following describes an expression of favor or disfavor for a person, place, thing, or event?**

    A. Attitude

    B. Belief

    C. Cognition

    D. Drive

    E. Behavior

The answer is A.
The definition of an attitude is "an expression of favor or disfavor for a person, place, thing, or event."

2. **Which of the following is a theory by Ajzen and Fishbein that outlines a model for the prediction of behavioral intention?**

    A. Cognitive Dissonance Theory

    B. Social Judgment Theory

    C. Theory of Reasoned Action

    D. Information Integration Theory

    E. Congruity Theory

The answer is C.
Ajzen and Fishbein are known for developing the Theory of Reasoned Action, which outlines a model for the prediction of behavioral intention.

3.　According to Petty and Cacioppo's Elaboration Likelihood Model, when a person is persuaded by the likeability of a speaker, he or she is using which processing route?

　　A. Central

　　B. Heuristic

　　C. Peripheral

　　D. Systemic

　　E. None of the above

The answer is C.
Petty and Cacioppo's Elaboration Likelihood Model suggests that people process persuasive messages using one of two processing routes: the central route and the peripheral route. When a person is persuaded by thinking about the *content* of the message, such as the quality of the arguments and evidence presented, he or she is using the *central* route. When a person is persuaded by factors *other than the content of the message*, such as the likeability of the speaker, he or she is using the *peripheral* route.

4.　Which of the following psychologists coined the term *group dynamics* to describe the positive and negative forces within groups of people?

　　A. Maslow

　　B. Lewin

　　C. Freud

　　D. Pavlov

　　E. Skinner

The answer is B.
Kurt Lewin is known as the founder of Social Psychology. He was one of the first to study *group dynamics*, a term he coined himself. Maslow is known for his Hierarchy of Needs model. Freud is known for his psychodynamic theory. Pavlov is known for his work on classical conditioning.

5. **Which of the following "deals with how the social perceiver uses information to arrive at causal explanations for events?"**

   A. Cognitive Dissonance Theory

   B. Classical conditioning

   C. Psychoanalysis

   D. Attribution Theory

   E. Frequency Theory

The answer is D.
The question provides the definition of Attribution Theory, which "deals with how the social perceiver uses information to arrive at causal explanations for events." Cognitive Dissonance Theory focuses on how humans strive for internal consistency (having one's attitudes match his or her behaviors). Classical Conditioning is a type of learning. Psychoanalysis is a branch of psychology founded by Sigmund Freud. Frequency Theory is related to the study of hearing.

6. **Which of the following describes obedience?**

   A. The act of changing one's beliefs and attitudes to match those of other members of a social group

   B. The act of following orders without question because they come from a legitimate authority

   C. The act of adapting one's actions to another's wishes or rules

   D. The act of influencing another's attitudes, beliefs, or behaviors

   E. The act of establishing credibility and authority

The answer is B.
Obedience is "the act of following orders without question because they come from a legitimate authority."

7. **Paul is driving to work when another driver cuts him off in traffic. Paul begins shouting and pounding on the steering wheel. Paul is exhibiting _____.**

    A. passive aggression

    B. passivity

    C. instrumental aggression

    D. dissociative rage

    E. impulsive aggression

The answer is E.
Paul is clearly exhibiting aggressive behavior, but it does not go as far as dissociative rage. Impulsive aggression is marked by strong anger, emotional outbursts, and possible harm to another person. This is also known as hostile aggression. You can see impulsive aggression in Paul's behavior, as he is shouting and pounding the steering wheel. Instrumental aggression harms another person as a means to achieve an end goal (e.g., mugging someone or tackling someone in football). Passive aggression involves indirect expressions of hostility, such as through procrastination, sullenness, or repeated failure to accomplish tasks for which one is responsible.

8. **According to Maslow's Hierarchy of Needs, humans must satisfy their physiological needs before they will desire to satisfy which other category of needs?**

    A. Safety

    B. Belonging

    C. Esteem

    D. Self-actualization

    E. All of the above

The answer is E.
In Maslow's Hierarchy of Needs model, he suggests that humans must satisfy their physiological needs, such as for food, clothing, and shelter, before they will desire to satisfy any other needs, including all of the other needs listed here.

9. **Which of the following is considered a prosocial emotion?**

   A. Anger

   B. Sadness

   C. Shame

   D. Happiness

   E. Awe

The answer is C.
Prosocial emotions are emotions that drive us to behave in ways that benefit others and society. Shame is a prosocial emotion because it lets people know when they have broken social and/or moral norms. Shame drives people to correct their behavior to meet societal norms for appropriate and moral behavior.

10. **Which of the following statements is true of long-term memory?**

   A. Long-term memory has nearly infinite storage capacity.

   B. Long-term memory is also known as working memory.

   C. Long-term memory allows people to temporarily store and manipulate visual images.

   D. Long-term memory has a shorter duration than working memory.

   E. None of the above statements are true of long-term memory.

The answer is A.
This is the only statement in this set that is true of long-term memory.

11. **The term *chunking* refers to**

    A. transferring memories from short-term to long-term

    B. combining small bits of information into larger, familiar pieces

    C. sensory memory

    D. repeating information over and over to increase the duration of time in which it stays in short-term memory

    E. an organizational process for cataloguing memories

The answer B.
Chunking refers to the process of combining small bits of information into larger, familiar pieces. For example, someone might look at a bunch of broccoli, carrots, and cauliflower and think of them collectively as "vegetables."

12. **The smallest units of speech are called**

    A. vowels

    B. syllables

    C. phonemes

    D. semantic

    E. syntax

The answer is C.
The smallest units of speech are called *phonemes*. The other words are related to language, but they do not describe the smallest units of speech.

13. **Which of the following terms describes the process by which memories fade over time?**

    A. Memory loss

    B. Memory fade

    C. Memory decay

    D. Memory delay

    E. Memory recall

The answer is C.
The process by which memories fade over time is called *memory decay*. The other options are distractions.

14. **The study of psychology began in _____ and was established by _____.**

    A. The United States; Freud

    B. Germany; Freud

    C. Germany; Ebbinghaus

    D. The United States; Skinner

    E. France; Piaget

The answer is C.
The study of psychology began in Germany in the 1870s. Hermann Ebbinghaus is considered a founding father of the field.

15. Conduction aphasia is caused by which of the following?

    A. Disruptions in the connection between the Wernicke's and Broca's areas

    B. Disruptions in the ability to consolidate information at a neural level

    C. Short-term memory loss due to retrograde amnesia

    D. Blockage of neural circuits in working memory

    E. Damage to the cerebellum

The answer is A.
Conduction aphasia is a specific (and rare) type of aphasia. It is a disconnection between the areas of the brain responsible for speech comprehension (Wernicke's area) and speech production (Broca's area).

16. An experiment that produces identical results each time is considered which of the following?

    A. Valid, but not reliable

    B. Reliable, but not valid

    C. Valid and reliable

    D. Reliable with questionable validity

    E. Valid with questionable reliability

The answer is D.
In terms of research methodology and results, *reliability* is the degree to which an assessment tool or experiment produces stable and consistent results. An experiment that produces identical results is reliable. *Validity* refers to the degree to which a test measures what it is intended to measure. In this case, we know that the experiment produces reliable results, but we do not know anything about its validity.

17. The assumption that maladaptive thought patterns and behaviors are learned is associated with which of the following?

     A. Behavioral therapy

     B. Cognitive therapy

     C. Psychoanalytic therapy

     D. Rogerian therapy

     E. Group therapy

The answer is A.
Behavioral therapy assumes that maladaptive thought patterns and behaviors are learned and, thus, they can be replaced with new learned thoughts and behaviors. Therefore, a goal of behavioral therapy is to help patients learn new ways of thinking and behaving that offer better coping and functioning.

18. You have conducted two experiments in which you failed to get the same result although the conditions under which both experiments are identical. It is clear that the measurement lacks which of the following?

     A. Face validity

     B. Construct validity

     C. Inter-rater reliability

     D. Reliability

     E. Internal validity

The answer is D.
Reliability is the degree to which an assessment tool or experiment produces stable and consistent results. If you're conducting identical experiments, they should yield similar results. If they do not, the measurements are not reliable.

19. **When is punishment most effective is changing or suppressing behavior?**

    A. Punishment is most effective when it is delayed, inconsistent, and mild.

    B. Punishment is most effective when it is immediate, consistent, and intense.

    C. Punishment is most effective when it is explained.

    D. Punishment is most effective when it is immediate, consistent, and mild.

    E. Punishment is most effective when it is vague.

The answer is B.
Research on operant conditioning demonstrates that punishments are most effective in modifying behavior when they are immediate, consistent, and intense. In other words, punishments must occur immediately after the indiscretion. Punishments must also be administered consistently. Finally, to be most effective, punishments should be intense.

20. **A psychologist administers the same IQ test three times to the same subject and receives identical or similar results each time. However, many scholars argue that IQ tests do not measure intelligence, but rather measure one's test-taking ability. This suggests that IQ tests are which of the following?**

    A. Valid but not reliable

    B. Both valid and reliable

    C. Neither valid nor reliable

    D. Reliable but not valid

    E. Lacking internal reliability

The answer is D.
Reliability is the degree to which an assessment tool or experiment produces stable and consistent results. Validity refers to the degree to which a test measures what it is intended to measure. The prompt in this question is suggesting that IQ tests are reliable but not valid.

21. **Which of the following attempts to establish an unpleasant response to the object that produces an undesired behavior?**

    A. Systematic desensitization

    B. Implosion therapy

    C. Aversive classical conditioning

    D. Punishment

    E. Unconditioned stimulus

The answer is C.
Classical conditioning is a process of learning in which a natural response (e.g., salivating) to a potent stimulus (e.g., food) comes to be elicited in response to a previously neutral stimulus (e.g., bell). This happens by repeated pairings of the unconditioned stimulus and the conditioned stimulus. Over time, the conditioned stimulus is able to produce the same response (i.e., conditioned response) as the unconditioned stimulus. Aversive classical conditioning is a type of behavior modification that seeks to reduce a undesired behavior by establishing an unpleasant response to that behavior.

22. **The ability to imitate the behavior of others and perform the same behavior under the same or similar conditions describes which of the following?**

    A. Modeling

    B. Shaping

    C. Imitation

    D. Reinforcement

    E. Play

The answer is A.
The definition of modeling is "the ability to imitate the behavior of others and perform the same behavior under the same or similar conditions." The other choices are distractions from the correct term for this definition.

23. **Which approach to psychology suggests that people are controlled by their environments?**

    A. Humanism

    B. Behaviorism

    C. Psychodynamic

    D. Cognitive

    E. Biological

The answer is B.
The behaviorist approach suggests that people are controlled by their environments. The humanist approach considers the entire person and emphasizes humans' drive for self-actualization. The psychodynamic approach looks at the forces that drive human behavior and emotion. Cognitive psychology examines mental processes, such as attention, thinking, memory, language, and learning. The biological approach studies the physiological, developmental, and genetic mechanisms that drive behavior.

24. **Which of the following statements best describes the evolutionary perspective of psychology?**

    A. The evolutionary approach explains human behavior in terms of classical and operational conditioning.

    B. The evolutionary approach studies the effects of genes on human behavior.

    C. The evolutionary approach seeks to understand the function of different mental processes.

    D. The evolutionary approach explains human behavior in terms of the selective pressures that shape behavior.

    E. The evolutionary approach seeks to study the whole person.

The answer is D.
Choice A is describing behaviorism. Choice B is describing biological psychology. Choice C is describing cognitive psychology. Choice E is describing humanism.

25. **Which of the following psychologist founded the psychodynamic perspective of psychology?**

    A. Sigmund Freud

    B. Ivan Pavlov

    C. B. F. Skinner

    D. Abraham Maslow

    E. Carl Rogers

The answer is A.
Pavlov and Skinner were behaviorists. Maslow and Rogers were humanists.

26. **Jane's experiment did not produce significant results and she is afraid that her paper will not get published. She decides to change some of the numbers in her data to get the outcome she desired. Jane has violated which general principle of ethics, according to the APA?**

    A. Beneficence

    B. Fidelity

    C. Responsibility

    D. Justice

    E. Integrity

The answer is E.
The integrity principle of ethics, according to the APA, requires researchers to report their findings accurately and honestly.

27. **With which of the following research methods does the observer have direct contact with the group he or she is observing?**

    A. Field experiment

    B. Participant observation

    C. Laboratory experiment

    D. Natural observation

    E. Controlled observation

The answer is B.
The participant observer study design allows researchers to blend in with the group of people they are studying.

28. **The requirement that researchers explain to potential participants the purpose and nature of a study, as well as any possible risks associated with participation, is known as**

    A. informed consent

    B. integrity

    C. researcher responsibility

    D. liability

    E. confidentiality

The answer is A.
Informed consent tells potential participants the purpose and nature of a study, as well as any potential risks, before they engage in it.

29. **Which of the following topics do cognitive psychologists study?**

    A. Behavior

    B. Emotion

    C. Self-actualization

    D. Memory and learning

    E. Genes and DNA

The answer is D.
Cognitive psychologists study mental processes such as thought, memory, learning, language, and attention.

30. **Which of the following psychologists can be categorized as a humanist?**

    A. Sigmund Freud

    B. Ivan Pavlov

    C. B. F. Skinner

    D. Abraham Maslow

    E. Wilhelm Wundt

The answer is D.
Abraham Maslow is the only humanist among these choices.

31. **Which of the following prevents a person from moving while experiencing dreams?**

    A. REM atonia

    B. NREM sleep

    C. Muscle relaxers

    D. Beta waves

    E. Alpha waves

The answer is A.
Dreams most often occur during REM sleep. REM atonia keeps people from moving while experiencing dreams.

32. **During the beginning of sleep, when a person is still relatively awake, the brain produces**

    A. Rapid Eye Movement

    B. Beta Waves

    C. Alpha waves

    D. Hallucinations

    E. None of the above

The answer is B.
Beta waves are those associated with wakefulness.

33.   Dreaming most often occurs during which phase of sleep?

A.   Stage 1 (theta waves)

B.   Stage 2 (sleep spindles)

C.   Stage 3 (delta waves)

D.   Stage 4 (REM)

E.   Dreaming occurs in all of the above stages

The answer is D.
Dreams most often occur during REM sleep (Stage 4).

34.   Which of the following is NOT considered a benefit of meditation?

A.   Greater capacity for empathy

B.   Decreased stress

C.   Increased anxiety

D.   Increased gray matter in the brain

E.   Improved sleep

The answer is C.
Meditation offers a host of benefits and it is especially helpful in reducing anxiety. It is not known to *increase* anxiety.

35. **Research on sleep provides evidence to support the ideas that**

    A. sleep is not necessary in the production of brain proteins

    B. all individuals require at least 8 hours of sleep each night for optimal functioning

    C. low-quality sleep and sleep deprivation negatively impact mood

    D. sleep does not impact learning

    E. sleep is not essential to well-being

The answer is C.
The other statements are inaccurate.

36. **A dog learns that when it rings a bell, its owner will let it outside. This is an example of which kind of learning?**

    A. Modeling

    B. Classical conditioning

    C. Instrumental conditioning

    D. Stimulus control

    E. Operant conditioning

The answer is E.
Operant conditioning is sometimes called *instrumental learning*. It involves learning through trial and consequences. Reinforcements and punishments are core tools through which operant behavior modification occurs. In this case, the dog learns that the behavior of ringing a bell is rewarded by its owner opening the door.

37. **Which of the following types of learning involves reinforcement and punishment?**

    A. Operant conditioning

    B. Classical conditioning

    C. Habituation

    D. Instrumental conditioning

    E. Modeling

The answer is A.
Operant conditioning is sometimes called *instrumental learning*. It involves learning through trial and consequences, as well as rewards and punishments.

38. **Which of the following types of learning involves a stimulus and response?**

    A. Operant conditioning

    B. Classical conditioning

    C. Habituation

    D. Instrumental conditioning

    E. Modeling

The answer is B.
Classical conditioning is a process of learning in which a natural response (e.g., salivating) to a potent stimulus (e.g., food) comes to be elicited in response to a previously neutral stimulus (e.g., bell). This happens by repeated pairings of the unconditioned stimulus and the conditioned stimulus. Over time, the conditioned stimulus is able to produce the same response (i.e., conditioned response) as the unconditioned stimulus.

39. **Which of the following depicts Freud's stages of psychosexual development in the correct order?**

    A. Oral, phallic, anal, latent, genital

    B. Genital, phallic, anal, latent, oral

    C. Phallic, oral, anal, genital, latent

    D. Oral, anal, phallic, latent, genital

    E. Anal, oral, latent, phallic, genital

The answer is D.
The correct order of the stages of psychosexual development are: oral, anal, phallic, latent, and genital.

40. **According to Piaget, the sensorimotor stage occurs between which ages?**

    A. 0-2 years

    B. 2-7 years

    C. 7-11 years

    D. 11-15 years

    E. 15+ years

The answer is A.
The sensorimotor stage occurs between ages 0 and 2.

41. **Piaget's theory of cognitive development is concerned with which population?**

    A. Newborn babies

    B. Children of all ages

    C. Young adults

    D. Mature adults

    E. Elderly adults

The answer is B.
Piaget's theory of cognitive development is concerned with children of all ages.

42. **Which theory explains how parent-child relationships emerge and influence subsequent development?**

    A. Psychoanalytic theory

    B. Social learning theory

    C. Cognitive development

    D. Attachment theory

    E. None of the above

The answer is D.
Attachment theory examines the influence that parent-child relationships have on future relational and personal development.

43. **Developmental psychologists often prefer which type of research design?**

    A. Experimental

    B. Participant observation

    C. Case study

    D. Cross-sectional

    E. Longitudinal

The answer is E.
Longitudinal designs allow researchers because these to study the same people repeatedly over long periods of time, which increases the accuracy of any observed changes.

44. **On which level of Kohlberg's moral stages is a child whose morality is based on rules and punishments?**

    A. Level I. Pre-conventional/premoral

    B. Level II: Conventional/Role conformity

    C. Level III: Post-conventional/Self-accepted moral principles

    D. Level IV: Fully moral

    E. None of the above

The answer is A.
On Level I of Kohlnerg's moral stages (the pre-conventional/premoral stage), children's sense of morality is based on the rules they are given as well as punishments that are doled out for breaking those rules.

45. **Which of the following disorders is characterized by hallucinations and delusions such as hearing voices?**

    A. Depression

    B. Obsessive compulsive disorder

    C. Bipolar disorder

    D. Schizophrenia

    E. Mania

The answer is D.
Schizophrenia is the only one of the listed disorders that is characterized by hallucinations and delusions.

46. **Which of the following drugs has stimulant and hallucinogenic effects?**

    A. Molly

    B. Adderall

    C. Marijuana

    D. Cocaine

    E. Pain killers

The answer is A.
Molly is a powder form of the drug MDMA. It is the only drug listed in this series that has both stimulant and hallucinogenic effects.

47. **Jimmy is experiencing recurring negative thoughts, a loss of interest in activities that used to excite him, trouble sleeping, and a loss of appetite. From which of the following disorders is Jimmy most likely suffering?**

    A. Depression

    B. Obsessive compulsive disorder

    C. Bipolar disorder

    D. Schizophrenia

    E. Mania

The answer is A.
The symptoms listed are classic symptoms of depression.

48. **Which of the following anxiety disorders is characterized by a fear of losing control, being trapped, or panicking in public places?**

    A. Acrophrobia

    B. Agoraphobia

    C. Generalized anxiety disorder

    D. Post-traumatic stress disorder

    E. General panic attack

The answer is B.
Agoraphobia is characterized by a fear of losing control, being trapped, or panicking in public places. People with this disorder are often afraid to leave their homes.

49. **Antidepressants are often associated with which of the following side effects?**

    A. Insomnia

    B. Dry mouth

    C. An increase in suicidal thoughts

    D. Decreased sexual drive and function

    E. All of the above

The answer is E.
All of the side effects listed are associated with antidepressants.

50. **Which of the following types of disorders is characterized by real physical symptoms that cannot be fully explained by a medical condition, the effects of a drug, or another mental disorder?**

    A. Personality disorders

    B. Anxiety disorders

    C. Somatoform disorders

    D. Affective disorders

    E. Dissociative disorders

The answer is C.
People with somatoform disorders experience real symptoms that cannot be fully explained by a medical condition, mental disorder, or drug. Hypochondria is a type of somatoform disorder. People with hypochondria believe they have an illness when there are no objective signs of that illness present. They often diagnose themselves with illnesses and do not believe doctors who disagree with their diagnoses.

51. **Which of the following personality disorders is characterized by an exaggerate sense of self- importance, a strong desire to be admired, and a lack of empathy?**

   A. Borderline personality disorder

   B. Histrionic personality disorder

   C. Avoidant personality disorder

   D. Narcissistic personality disorder

   E. Antisocial personality disorder

The answer is D.
The only one of the listed disorders that is characterized by an exaggerated sense of self, a strong desire to be admired, and a lack of empathy is the narcissistic personality disorder.

52. **People with which of the following personality disorders often lack empathy and remorse, and exhibit aggressive, impulsive, reckless, or irresponsible behavior?**

   A. Borderline personality disorder

   B. Histrionic personality disorder

   C. Avoidant personality disorder

   D. Narcissistic personality disorder

   E. Antisocial personality disorder

The answer is E.
Antisocial personality disorder is marked by a lack of empathy and remorse, as well as aggressive, impulsive, reckless, or irresponsible behavior.

53. **A person who experiences depressive and manic episodes may have which of the following disorders?**

    A. Depression

    B. Obsessive compulsive disorder

    C. Bipolar disorder

    D. Schizophrenia

    E. Mania

The answer is C.
Bipolar disorder is characterized by episodes of depression as well as manic episodes. Sufferers of bipolar disorder are sometimes referred to as *manic-depressives* for this reason.

54. **Hypochondria is an example of which of the following types of disorders?**

    A. Personality disorders

    B. Anxiety disorders

    C. Somatoform disorders

    D. Affective disorders

    E. Dissociative disorders

The answer is C.
Hypochondria is a type of somatoform disorder. People with somatoform disorders experience real symptoms that cannot be fully explained by a medical condition, mental disorder, or drug. People with hypochondria believe they have an illness when there are no objective signs of that illness present. They often diagnose themselves with illnesses and do not believe doctors who disagree with their diagnoses.

55. The _____ nervous system prepares the body for action, while the _____ nervous system keeps the body still.

    A. Sympathetic, parasympathetic

    B. Autonomic, sympathetic

    C. Parasympathetic, autonomic

    D. Sympathetic, autonomic

    E. Parasympathetic, sympathetic

The answer is A.

The sympathetic nervous system prepares the body for action, while the parasympathetic nervous system keeps the body still. These systems together make up the autonomic nervous system.

56. Which of the following theories of emotion suggests that people experience emotions because they perceive physiological changes in their bodies?

    A. Cognitive appraisal

    B. Schachter and Singer's Two-Factor Theory

    C. Evolutionary Theory

    D. James-Lange Theory

    E. Cannon-Bard Theory

The answer is D.

The James-Lange Theory suggests that people experience emotions because they perceive physiological changes in their bodies. In other words, humans feel changes in their bodies and then their brains react to those changes. Reactions to the physiological changes constitute emotions.

57. **Which of the following terms describes a theoretical construct that is used to explain the reasons for people's actions, desires, and needs?**

   A. Emotion

   B. Empathy

   C. Motivation

   D. Hunger

   E. Thirst

The answer is C.
The term *motivation* is used to describe the reasons for people's actions, desires, and needs, including hunger and thirst. The other answers are distractions.

58. **Which of the following is an example of intrinsic motivation?**

   A. Money

   B. Receiving an award

   C. Feeling a sense of accomplishment

   D. Winning a prize

   E. A cheering crowd

The answer is C.
Intrinsic motivation comes from within a person. Examples of intrinsic motivation include autonomy, a sense of accomplishment, mastery of a skill, and curiosity. Extrinsic motivation is external to the person, such as external rewards like trophies, awards, money, or prizes.

59. **Which of the following drugs is commonly abused by college students because its stimulant effects can aid in studying?**

    A. Cocaine

    B. Marijuana

    C. Adderall

    D. Alcohol

    E. All of the above

The answer is C.
Adderall is prescribed to treat ADHD. It contains a combination of amphetamine and dextroamphetamine, which are stimulants that affect the chemicals in the brain that contribute to hyperactivity and impulse control.

60. **Which of the following theories suggests that we are motivated to take action based on our biological needs?**

    A. Drive reduction theory

    B. Arousal theory

    C. Instinct theory

    D. Maslow's Hierarchy of Needs

    E. Goal-setting theory

The answer is A.
Drive reduction theory states that humans are motivated to take action to satisfy biological or physical needs.

61. **Which of the following theories of emotion argues that one's experience of emotion depends on their physiological arousal and cognitive interpretation of that arousal?**

    A. Cognitive appraisal

    B. Schachter and Singer's Two-Factor Theory

    C. Evolutionary Theory

    D. James-Lange Theory

    E. Cannon-Bard Theory

The answer is B.
Schacter and Singer's Two-Factor Theory says that one's emotional experience is based on two factors: physiological arousal and a label of that arousal. In other words, people's emotional experiences come from physiological feelings (i.e., changes in the body such as increased heart rate, shallow breathing, and sweating) and the labels we assign to those feelings (i.e., sadness, fear, anger).

62. **Which of the following is the correct term for vision that comes from the side of the eye?**

    A. Peripheral vision

    B. Tunnel vision

    C. Perceptive vision

    D. Sensation

    E. Detection

The answer is A.
Peripheral vision is a part of vision that occurs outside the center of one's gaze. Peripheral sight comes from the outer sides of the field of vision.

63. **Which of the following correctly lists Paiget's stages of cognitive development?**

A. Sensorimotor, concrete operational, preoperational, formal operational

B. Preoperational, formal operational, concrete operational. sensorimotor

C. Formal operational, concrete operational, preoperational, sensorimotor

D. Concrete operational, preoperational, sensorimotor, formal operational

E. Sensorimotor, preoperational, concrete operational, formal operational

The answer is E.
The correct order of Piaget's stages of cognitive development is: Sensorimotor, preoperational, concrete operational, formal operational.

64. **Which of the following therapies is considered a last resort method of treating depression when all other therapies have failed?**

A. Antidepressant medication

B. Psychoanalytic therapy

C. Cognitive-behavioral therapy

D. Electroconvulsive shock therapy

E. Group therapy

The answer is D.
Electroconvulsive shock therapy is considered a last resort method of treating aggressive clinical depression. Psychoanalytic theory is not widely practiced, nor is it commonly prescribed for the treatment of depression. Common treatments for depression include group therapy, cognitive-behavioral therapy, and antidepressant medication.

65. Which of the following best describes a cross-sectional study?

    A. A researcher follows the same participants over a period of time.

    B. A researcher examines different groups of people who share one or more similar characteristics.

    C. A researcher brings people into a lab and has them complete a task.

    D. A researcher observes people in their homes.

    E. A researcher surveys observes people in public.

The answer is B.
A cross-sectional study is one where a researcher examines different groups of people who share one or more similar characteristics, such as age, IQ, or geographical location.

66. Psychology researchers use which of the following terms to describe thinking, reasoning, and solving problems?

    A. Emotion

    B. Intuition

    C. Perception

    D. Sensation

    E. Cognition

The answer is E.
Cognition is the mental process of acquiring knowledge and understanding through thought, experience, and the senses. Cognition includes mental processes such as thinking, reasoning, and problem-solving.

67. **Lawrence Kohlberg is known for his research in the area of _____ development.**

    A. Cognitive

    B. Moral

    C. Personality

    D. Emotional

    E. Physical

The answer is B.
Lawrence Kohlberg is known for his research in the area of moral development.

68. **Which of the following statements about antidepressants do most psychology researchers and practitioners consider true?**

    A. Antidepressants are helpful in treating some forms of depression.

    B. For many patients, antidepressants are less helpful than individual therapy in treating depression.

    C. Antidepressants alone are not enough to successfully treat depression in many patients.

    D. All of the above

    E. None of the above

The answer is D.
Choices A, B, and C are all statements about antidepressants that most psychology researchers and practitioners would consider true.

69. **Which of the following therapies helps people work through problems by interacting with one or more therapists as well as other individuals experiencing similar struggles?**

    A. Individual therapy

    B. Drug therapy

    C. Group therapy

    D. Psychoanalytic therapy

    E. Social-Emotional therapy

The answer is C.
Group therapy brings together one or more therapists with multiple individuals who are experiencing similar struggles. None of the other theories listed here are conducted in a group setting.

70. **According to Kübler-Ross, the correct order of the stages of grief are:**

    A. denial, anger, bargaining, depression, acceptance.

    B. anger, denial, depression, bargaining, acceptance.

    C. denial, depression, anger, acceptance, bargaining.

    D. depression, denial, anger, bargaining, acceptance.

    E. acceptance, denial, anger, bargaining, depression.

The answer is A.
According to Kübler-Ross, the stages of grief (in order) are: denial, anger, bargaining, depression, and acceptance.

71. **Which of the following correctly describes the difference between depression and grief?**

    A. Grief often entails a sense of worthlessness whereas depression does not.

    B. Grief involves excessive guilt and depression does not.

    C. Grief lasts longer than major depression.

    D. Grief subsides after a period of time whereas depression often persists for extended periods of time.

    E. Grief is a clinical condition whereas depression is a normal, healthy emotion.

The answer is D.
Grief is a normal, healthy emotion. Depression is a clinical illness. When processed in a normal, healthy way, grief lasts for a period of time and subsides on its own. However, prolonged grief can lead to depression, which is an ongoing mental illness. Depression persists for extended periods of time whereas grief is shorter-lived.

72. **Cara describes herself as outgoing, funny and friendly. These characteristics are part of her**

    A. self-esteem.

    B. motivation.

    C. self-concept.

    D. group identity.

    E. physique.

The answer is C.
Self-concept is a collection of one's beliefs about him or herself. It includes beliefs about one's personality, gender and sexual identities, academic performance, and racial identity, among other characteristics.

73. **In personality research, which of the following describes personal characteristics that are biologically determined?**

   A. Nature

   B. Environment

   C. State

   D. Trait

   E. Ego

The answer is D.
Personal characteristics that are determined by biology are called traits.

74. **Which of the following is not a standard method used to assess personality?**

   A. Self-reports

   B. Observer-reports

   C. Test data

   D. Projective measures

   E. Laboratory study

The answer is E.
Laboratory studies are not commonly used to assess personality. All of the other research methods listed here are frequently used to assess personality.

75.   The Big Five personality traits are:

   A. Humor, openness, extraversion, agreeableness, neuroticism.

   B. Extraversion, agreeableness, enlightenment, openness, neuroticism

   C. Openness, conscientiousness, extraversion, agreeableness, neuroticism.

   D. Extraversion, introversion, humor, neuroticism, openness

   E. Happiness, neuroticism, shyness, openness, extraversion

The answer is C.
The Big Five personality Traits are: Openness, conscientiousness, extraversion, agreeableness, and neuroticism.

76.   _____ refers to the pattern of thoughts, feelings, social adjustments and behaviors consistently exhibited over time.

   A. Preferences

   B. Self-esteem

   C. Construct

   D. Personality

   E. Extraversion

The answer is D.
The definition of personality is the pattern of thoughts, feelings, social adjustments and behaviors consistently exhibited over time.

77. **Conscientiousness refers to one's**

    A. tendency to be creative, curious, and open to new ideas.

    B. tendency to be organized and self-disciplined.

    C. tendency to experience unpleasant emotions easily.

    D. tendency to be compassionate and cooperative towards others.

    E. tendency to exhibit to seek stimulation in the company of others.

The answer is B.
Conscientiousness refers to one's tendency be organized and self-disciplined.

78. **Which of the following types of psychologists believe that one's personality consists of learned patterns**

    A. Emotional psychologists

    B. Humanists

    C. Behavioral psychologists

    D. Psychoanalytic theorists

    E. Cognitive psychologists

The answer is C.
Behavioral psychologists believe that one's personality consists of learned patterns.

79. **Kim lives in Alaska and says that a 60-degree day is warm. Steve lives in Arizona and thinks 60-degree weather is cold. Their perceptions differ because of**

    A. their frame of reference

    B. where they place their attention

    C. perceptual constancy

    D. their personalities

    E. their top-down processing

The answer is A.
Kim and Steve have differing frames of reference, which account for their different opinions about how cold or warm 60-degree weather is.

80. **Which of the following terms explains why roads appear to converge in the distance?**

    A. Light and shadow

    B. Continuing patterns

    C. Texture gradient

    D. Linear perspective

    E. None of the above

The answer is D.
In linear perspective, parallel lines that recede into the distance appear to get closer together. This explains why roads appear to converge in the distance.

81. **Anything that can be perceived with one of the five senses is considered _____ stimulus, whereas _____ stimulus refers to the specific object upon which one is focused.**

  A. Attended, environmental

  B. Image, recognition

  C. Environmental, attended

  D. Neural, retinal

  E. Neural, image

The answer is C.
Environmental stimuli are anything that can be perceived with the five senses. The specific object upon which one's attention is focused is called *attended stimuli*.

82. **An image on the retina of the eye is transformed into electrical signals in a process known as which of the following?**

  A. Transcendence

  B. Abduction

  C. Transformation

  D. Intensification

  E. Transduction

The answer is E.
Transduction is the process by which our eyes turn light into neural impulses that our brains can understand. Transduction takes an image on the retina of the eye and transforms it into electrical signals that the brain can process.

83. **Which of the following is true of secondary reinforcers?**

    A. They are learned.

    B. They are ineffective.

    C. They are more effective than primary reinforcers.

    D. They are innate.

    E. They are natural.

The answer is A.
Primary reinforcers occur naturally and do not need to be learned; they have biological and evolutionary bases. Examples of primary reinforcers include food, air, water, sleep, and sex. Secondary reinforcers involve stimuli that are rewarding because they have been paired with another, naturally-occurring reinforcer. Secondary reinforcers are learned.

84. **The analysis of information starting with features and building into a complete perception is known as which of the following?**

    A. Perceptual constancy

    B. Top-down processing

    C. Bottom-up processing

    D. Chunking

    E. Linking

The answer is C.
Bottom-up processing starts with features and builds up into a complete perception. Top-down processing starts with a perception (i.e., cognition) and then moves down to the senses, or specific features.

85. **Which of the following allows humans to perceive the world in three dimensions?**

A. Depth perception

B. Sensation

C. Disparity

D. Convergence

E. Accommodation

The answer is A.
Depth perception allows humans to see in three dimensions. The other choices are distractions.

86. **Neurons are made up of which of the following?**

A. Anterior cell, posterior cell, axon

B. Dendrite, soma, axon

C. Cell body, cell wall, nucleus

D. Myelin, dendrite, cell wall

E. None of the above

The answer is B.
Neurons are made up of dendrites, a soma, and axon. Dendrites are the treelike structures that receive signals from other nerve cells. The cell body, or soma, produces all of the proteins that make up all of the parts of the neuron. The axon is the main conducting component of the neuron; it transmits electrical signals throughout the nervous system.

87. **Which of the following describes the main function of myelin?**

    A. Myelin forms a protective coating over nerve axons.

    B. Myelin decreases the speed with which information travels from nerve cell to nerve cell.

    C. Myelin blocks reception of acetylcholine.

    D. Myelin slows down nerve degeneration.

    E. Myelin aids in the transference of neurotransmitters.

The answer is A.

The function of myelin is to protect the nerve axons. Myelin forms a protective coating over nerve axons.

88. **Neurotransmitters are released at which part of a cell?**

    A. Dendrite

    B. Axon terminal

    C. Nucleus

    D. Soma

    E. Myelin

The answer is B.

Neurotransmitters are released at the axon terminal.

89. Communication within a neuron is a(n) _____ process, while communication between neurons is a(n) _____ process.

    A. Chemical; mechanical

    B. Electrical; mechanical

    C. Chemical; electrical

    D. Electrical; chemical

    E. Mechanical; electrical

The answer is D.
Communication within a neuron is an electrical process, while communication between neurons is a chemical process.

90. Human behavior is influenced by genetic processes as well their environments and experiences. In psychology, this is known as which of the following?

    A. Genes versus experience

    B. Heredity versus environment

    C. Climate versus science

    D. Nature versus nurture

    E. Genes versus personality

The answer is D.
Psychologists use the phrase *nature versus nurture* to describe how human behavior is influenced by genetic characteristics as well as people's environments and experiences.

91. **Which of the following is the main link between the brain and the glandular system in the human body?**

    A. Hypothalamus

    B. Prefrontal cortex

    C. Central nervous system

    D. Sympathetic nervous system

    E. Parasympathetic nervous system

The answer is A.
The hypothalamus is the main link between the brain and the glandular system in the human body. The hypothalamus is responsible for activities of the autonomic nervous system.

92. **The endocrine system is responsible for which of the following functions?**

    A. It pumps blood throughout the body.

    B. It brings oxygen into the body.

    C. It secretes hormones into the blood stream for communication between cells.

    D. It processes sensory information from the eyes and ears.

    E. None of the above.

The answer is C.
The endocrine system is responsible for producing and regulating hormones. The endocrine system secretes hormones into the blood system for communication between cells.

93. An EEG records which of the following?

A. The electrical rhythm of the heart.

B. Electrical impulses from the brain.

C. Hormone secretion in the bloodstream.

D. Electrical currents in the body.

E. The number of neurons in the brain.

The answer is B.
EEG stands for electroencephalogram, which is a test that detects electrical activity in the brain.

94. In Pavlov's famous experiment, the dog's salivation over food was considered which of the following?

A. Conditioned response

B. Conditioned stimulus

C. Automatic stimulus

D. Unconditioned response

E. Unconditioned stimulus

The answer is D.
Dogs naturally salivate in response to food. They do not need to learn this response. Salivating is an unconditioned response to food (an unconditioned stimulus).

95. **Which of the following scientists is known for studying operant conditioning?**

A. Pavlov

B. Freud

C. Maslow

D. Piaget

E. Skinner

The answer is E.
B. F. Skinner is known for his work on operant conditioning. Operant conditioning is sometimes called *instrumental learning*. It involves learning through trial and consequences. Reinforcements and punishments are core tools through which behavior modification occurs.

Description of the Examination

The Introductory Sociology examination is designed to assess an individual's knowledge of the material typically presented in a one-semester introductory sociology course at most colleges and universities. The examination emphasizes basic facts and concepts as well as general theoretical approaches used by sociologists. Highly specialized knowledge of the subject and the methodology of the discipline is not required or measured by the test content.

The examination contains approximately 100 questions to be answered in 90 minutes. Some of these are pretest questions that will not be scored. Any time candidates spend on tutorials and providing personal information is in addition to the actual testing time.

Knowledge and Skills Required

Questions on the Introductory Sociology examination require candidates to demonstrate one or more of the following abilities. Some questions may require more than one of these abilities.

- Identification of specific names, facts, and concepts from sociological literature
- Understanding of relationships between concepts, empirical generalizations, and theoretical propositions of sociology
- Understanding the methods by which sociological relationships are established
- Application of concepts, propositions, and methods to hypothetical situations
- Interpretation of tables and charts

The subject matter of the Introductory Sociology examination is drawn from the following topics. The percentages next to the main topics indicate the approximate percentage of exam questions on that topic.

20%   **Institutions**
- Economic
- Educational
- Family
- Medical
- Political
- Religious

10%   **Social Patterns**
- Community
- Demography
- Human ecology
- Rural/urban patterns

25%   **Social Processes**
- Collective behavior and social movements
- Culture
- Deviance and social control
- Social change
- Social interaction
- Socialization

25%   **Social Stratification**
- Aging
- Power and inequality
- Professions and occupations
- Sex and gender roles
- Social class
- Social mobility

20%   **The Sociological Perspective**
- History of sociology
- Methods
- Sociological Theory

SAMPLE TEST

DIRECTIONS: Read each item and select the best response.

1. **Karl Marx is considered the founder of:**

   A. Structural Functionalism

   B. Rational Choice Theory

   C. Conflict Theory

   D. Racial Formation Theory

   E. Symbolic Interactionism

2. **A process where affluent people (often white) move into urban areas and displace the original lower-income residents (often people of color) is known as:**

   A. Gentrification

   B. Urban decay

   C. White flight

   D. Environmental racism

   E. Steering

3. **The practice of placing students in higher and lower-level curriculum groups based on test scores, grades, and/ or teacher discretion is known as:**

   A. The hidden curriculum

   B. Accomplishment of natural growth

   C. Stereotype threat

   D. Tracking

   E. The hidden threat

4. **Sociologists often use samples to make inferences about a population. The most important quality of a sample is that it is:**

   A. It is easy to conduct

   B. It is inexpensive

   C. It is large

   D. It includes people who do not wish to participate

   E. It is representative of the population

5. In the United States, it is usually considered rude not to make direct eye contact when talking to another person. Making eye contact is therefore an example of a:

    A. Right

    B. Taboo

    C. Norm

    D. Value

    E. Law

6. The process by which we learn how to become members of social and cultural groups is:

    A. Learning

    B. Socialization

    C. Gendering

    D. Societization

    E. Culturalization

7. Failing to cover your mouth when you sneeze is a violation of a:

    A. Taboo

    B. More

    C. Health code

    D. Law

    E. Folkway

8. Sarah is a sociologist studying roller derbies. To collect data she joins a roller derby team. Sarah is conducting a(n):

    A. Survey

    B. Experiment

    C. Content analysis

    D. Ethnography

    E. Natural experiment

9. The theory that views society as an organism in which all parts work together to promote stability is:

    A. Structural Functionalism

    B. Conflict Theory

    C. Symbolic Interactionism

    D. Structuralism

    E. Social Bonding Theory

10. Imagine you wanted to use the sociological imagination to understand depression. To do so, you might consider how an individual's likelihood of experiencing depression is related to:

    A. Personality

    B. Family income

    C. Use of anti-depressants

    D. Genetics

    E. Psychological history

11. When a group of people share a language, values, and a history they are referred to as a(n):

    A. Racial group

    B. Subculture

    C. Family

    D. Tribe

    E. Ethnic group

12. Social mobility happens most frequently in a:

    A. Social class system

    B. Caste system

    C. Feudal system

    D. Slavery system

    E. Royal system

13. Which of the following is NOT a dimension of social class?

    A. Wealth

    B. Income

    C. Race

    D. Educational Attainment

    E. Prestige

14. **Which of the following is NOT an example of a social movement?**

    A. The Civil Rights Movement

    B. The Gay Rights Movement

    C. Feminism

    D. Roe v. Wade

    E. The Pro-Life Movement

15. **Women often do not reach the upper ranks of corporations due to an invisible barrier known as:**

    A. The glass escalator

    B. The glass ceiling

    C. Sexism

    D. Discrimination

    E. Racism

16. **Most women in the United States take their husband's last name when they marry. This is evidence that the United States is:**

    A. Matrilineal

    B. Patrilineal

    C. Patriarchal

    D. Matriarchal

    E. Egalitarian

17. **Which of the following terms refers to the belief that an individual's successes and failures in life are solely a result of effort, intelligence, and ability?**

    A. Stratification

    B. Class privilege

    C. Ideology

    D. The myth of meritocracy

    E. Color-blind racism

18. **"I am never asked to speak for all the people of my racial group" is an example of:**

    A. White privilege

    B. Class privilege

    C. Male privilege

    D. Structural inequality

    E. Color-blind racism

19. **Who claimed that society is composed of two opposing social classes – the bourgeoisie and the proletariat?**

    A. C. Wright Mills

    B. Karl Marx

    C. Max Weber

    D. Emile Durkheim

    E. Auguste Comte

20. **Who is considered the founder of sociology?**

    A. C. Wright Mills

    B. Karl Marx

    C. Max Weber

    D. Emile Durkheim

    E. Auguste Comte

21. **According to Emile Durkheim's famous study on suicide, suicide rates are higher among the unmarried compared to the married. Durkheim argued that this was became unmarried people _____.**

    A. Are less happy than married people

    B. Are less likely to be prevented from committing suicide by a spouse

    C. Have weaker social ties

    D. Are less likely to have access to mental health care

    E. Are more likely to be Protestant

22. **Teenagers who participate in abstinence-only sex education programs have higher rates of teen pregnancy than teenagers who do not participant in these programs. According to Merton, a famous structural-functionalist, this is an example of a(n)_____.**

    A. Manifest function

    B. Latent function

    C. Accidental function

    D. Structural function

    E. Unexpected function

23. Which of the following theories posits that individuals act in ways that are based on meanings formed through social interaction with others?

  A. Structural Functionalism

  B. Rational Choice Theory

  C. Conflict Theory

  D. Racial Formation Theory

  E. Symbolic Interactionism

24. Ricardo tells a joke at a party and everyone stares blankly at him. He interprets their reactions to mean that he is not funny and in turn, worries that he is not a funny person. Ricardo's experience is an example of _____.

  A. The looking glass self

  B. Differentiation of the self

  C. Embarrassment

  D. Imitating others

  E. Taking the role of the other

25. An Asian American woman with a college degree whose parents are doctors is likely to marry an Asian American man with a college degree and whose parents are professionals. This pattern is an example of

  _____.

  A. Exogamy

  B. Monogamy

  C. Homogamy

  D. Patriarchy

  E. Propinquity

26. Emile Durkheim developed a term to refer to a mismatch between personal standards and larger social standards. This term is _____.

  A. Rebellion

  B. Socialization

  C. Group think

  D. Anomie

  E. Deviance

27. **When sociologists conduct experiments, they are attempting to isolate and measure the effect produced by a(n) _____.**

    A. Independent variable

    B. Dependent variable

    C. Confounding variable

    D. Mediating variable

    E. Moderating variable

28. **A positive correlation or association refers to when _____.**

    A. Variables stay the same

    B. Something good happens

    C. One variable goes up and another goes down

    D. Two variables move in opposite directions

    E. Two variables move in the same direction

29. **Rowan examined advertisements in magazines in order to understand the different ways that men and women are portrayed in advertisements. This is an example of a(n) _____.**

    A. Survey

    B. Experiment

    C. Content analysis

    D. Ethnography

    E. Natural experiment

30. **After the passage of Brown v. Board of Education of Topeka, there was a mass exodus of whites from racially-diverse urban areas to racially-homogenous suburbs. This process is: _____.**

    A. Gentrification

    B. Urban decay

    C. White flight

    D. Environmental racism

    E. Steering

31. **Rates of poverty in the United States are highest for which of the following groups?**

    A. The elderly

    B. Children under 18

    C. Unmarried men

    D. Married couple households

    E. Individuals who live in urban areas

32. **The fact that environmentally hazardous materials (e.g., toxic waste, pollution) are more likely to be located in low-income or minority communities is referred to as _____ .**

    A. Gentrification

    B. Urban decay

    C. White flight

    D. Environmental racism

    E. Environmental injustice

33. **The fact that, on average, non-white children go to schools with fewer resources compared to white children is an example of _____ .**

    A. Overt racism

    B. Covert racism

    C. Institutional racism

    D. Prejudice

    E. Segregation

34. **Which group has the lowest marriage rates in the United States?**

    A. White men

    B. Black men

    C. Hispanic men

    D. Hispanic women

    E. Black women

35. **According to Merton's strain theory, which type of deviance occurs when an individual accepts cultural goals (e.g., getting rich) but rejects the socially acceptable means of achieving them**

   A. Innovation

   B. Conformity

   C. Ritualism

   D. Retreatism

   E. Rebellion

36. **Sociologists believe that sex is _____ whereas gender is _____.**

   A. Socially constructed; biological

   B. Biological; socially constructed

   C. Relevant; irrelevant

   D. Irrelevant; relevant

   E. Mutable; immutable

37. **Over the past several decades, the U.S. economy has shifted from one based on _____ to one based on _____.**

   A. Services; manufacturing

   B. Manufacturing; goods

   C. Goods; manufacturing

   D. Manufacturing; services

   E. Finances; goods

38. **Which of the following statements about social mobility in the U.S. is false?**

   A. Anyone who works hard enough will achieve upward mobility

   B. Most social mobility happens within the middle class (e.g., from lower middle class to upper middle class)

   C. Most people remain in the same social class as their family of origin

   D. Educational attainment matters for social mobility

   E. Social mobility is usually related to societal-level factors, not individual ones

39. **If a new employee starts working at a faster pace than the other workers, this an example of**

    _____.

    A. Efficiency

    B. Division of labor

    C. Rate busting

    D. Loafing

    E. Rate setting

40. **We are just beginning to witness which of the following large-scale demographic shifts?**

    A. An increase in the divorce rate

    B. An increase in age at first marriage

    C. An increase in age at first birth

    D. An increase in the percentage of the population that is 65 and older

    E. An increase in stay-at-home mothers

41. **Which of the following demographic trends did NOT occur in the 20th century?**

    A. An increase in life expectancy

    B. Migration from urban to rural areas

    C. An increase in female-headed households

    D. An increase in the divorce rate

    E. An increase in the number of women in the labor force

42. **Urban ethnographic sociology emerged from:**

    A. The Chicago school

    B. The New York school

    C. The Harvard school

    D. The Emory school

    E. The Yale school

43. **Which famous sociologist argued that capitalism was a result of the Protestant ethic?**

    A. C. Wright Mills

    B. Karl Marx

    C. Max Weber

    D. Emile Durkheim

    E. Auguste Comte

44. **Which famous sociologist wrote about the power elite?**

    A. C. Wright Mills

    B. Karl Marx

    C. Max Weber

    D. Emile Durkheim

    E. Auguste Comte

45. **Which famous sociologist is considered the first academic sociologist?**

    A. C. Wright Mills

    B. Karl Marx

    C. Max Weber

    D. Emile Durkheim

    E. Auguste Comte

46. **Food deserts refer to:**

    A. Desert communities where there is too much food

    B. Desert communities with unhealthy foods

    C. Desert communities with not enough food

    D. Communities that lack access to fresh, healthy foods

    E. Communities without any restaurants

47. **Which sociological theory maintains that reality is based on culturally agreed upon meanings?**

    A. Rational choice theory

    B. Social constructionism

    C. Positivism

    D. Structural functionalism

    E. Conflict theory

48. **Which statement best describes trends in the economy since the 1970s?**

    A. Declining levels of income inequality

    B. Declining levels of wealth inequality

    C. Declining levels of income and wealth inequality

    D. Increasing levels of income inequality

    E. Increasing levels of income and wealth inequality

49. **What is the term used to describe a process by which human conditions become defined and treated as medical conditions?**

    A. Medicalization

    B. Mentalization

    C. Healthism

    D. Pathologism

    E. Deviation

50. **Which famous sociologist wrote extensively about bureaucracy?**

    A. C. Wright Mills

    B. Karl Marx

    C. Max Weber

    D. Emile Durkheim

    E. Auguste Comte

51. **The McDonaldization of society refers to:**

    A. The spread of McDonald's chains all over the globe

    B. A process by which cultural products become homogenous and predictable

    C. An increase in the number of fast food restaurants

    D. The rise in obesity rates

    E. The rise in the number of foods with preservatives

52. **Research that uses both qualitative and quantitative methods is known as:**

    A. Ethnography

    B. Participant observation

    C. Action research

    D. Experiments

    E. Mixed methods

53. **Quantitative methods are best for:**

    A. Exploratory research

    B. Collecting non-numerical data

    C. Confirming a hypothesis

    D. Generating a new theory

    E. Small sample sizes

54. **Research that attempts to understand the past is referred to as:**

    A. Experimental

    B. Survey research

    C. Ethnography

    D. Historical research

    E. Mixed methods

55. **Brianna moves from a small rural town in Pennsylvania to New York City. She is overwhelmed by the fast pace of life in New York. The term that best describes her experience is _____.**

   A. Culture shock

   B. Socialization

   C. The looking glass self

   D. Deviance

   E. Social control

56. **Which of the following is an example of a counterculture?**

   A. Catholics

   B. The Amish

   C. Nurses

   D. Athletes

   E. Latinos

57. **Which of the following is an example of an occupation in the secondary labor market?**

   A. Physician

   B. Professor

   C. Fast food worker

   D. Lawyer

   E. Plumber

58. **Which of the following statements about stratification is true?**

   A. All societies have equal levels of stratification

   B. All societies have some form of stratification

   C. Capitalist societies have less inequality than socialist ones

   D. Levels of stratification have not changed over time in the U.S.

   E. Social mobility is not possible in class-based societies

59. **Behaviors that violate social norms are referred to as _____.**

    A. Culture shock

    B. Socialization

    C. The looking glass self

    D. Deviance

    E. Social control

60. **Which institution is primarily responsible for reproducing members of society?**

    A. The family

    B. The economy

    C. Religion

    D. Education

    E. Politics

61. **What explanation does NOT explain why women are paid less than men?**

    A. Discrimination

    B. Men and women tend to have different occupations

    C. Men and women tend to have different specialties within occupations

    D. Women have primarily responsibility for childcare

    E. Women are less concerned with income

62. **The practice of women taking two or more husbands at a time is known as:**

    A. Monogamy

    B. Polygyny

    C. Polyandry

    D. Bigamy

    E. Bisexuality

63. Policies and practices that push schoolchildren (particularly low-income minorities) out of classrooms and into the criminal justice systems is referred to as:

   A. Out of place policing

   B. Steering

   C. Institutional racism

   D. The hidden curriculum

   E. The school-to-prison pipeline

64. Schools in the U.S. have dramatically different levels of resources, in part, because school funding at the local level comes primarily from:

   A. Income taxes

   B. Property taxes

   C. Sales taxes

   D. Donations

   E. Tax credits

65. Which group is NOT under-represented in the U.S. Congress?

   A. Women

   B. Latinos

   C. Whites

   D. African Americans

   E. Asian Americans

66. The process by which existing social roles and norms are altered or replaced by new ones is known as:

   A. Culture shock

   B. Socialization

   C. The looking glass self

   D. Resocialization

   E. Social control

67. A type of social movement that advocates for the restoration of a previous social arrangement (e.g., for the repeal of Roe v. Wade) is known as a _____ social movement.

   A. Reactionary

   B. Reformist

   C. Revolutionary

   D. Personal transformation

   E. Civil Rights

68. A process by which collective delusions of threats to society spread rapidly through a social group is known as _____.

   A. Social control

   B. Deviance

   C. Mass hysteria

   D. The bystander effect

   E. The looking glass self

69. A process by which individuals attempt to influence the perceptions of others is referred to as _____.

   A. Social control

   B. Deviance

   C. The bystander effect

   D. The looking glass self

   E. Impression management

70. The process by which individuals do not offer assistance to victims when other people are present is referred to as _____.

   A. Social control

   B. Deviance

   C. Mass hysteria

   D. The bystander effect

   E. The looking glass self

71. The Hispanic paradox is the name given to describe the fact that despite having lower average incomes than whites, Hispanics in the U.S. have _____ compared to whites.

    A. Higher levels of educational attainment

    B. Better health outcomes

    C. Larger families

    D. Higher marriage rates

    E. Fewer children

72. A medical sociologist would study all of the following topics EXCEPT:

    A. Mortality patterns

    B. Marriage and health

    C. Erectile dysfunction

    D. Cesarean sections

    E. Political candidates

73. Which of the following sociological terms refers to the capacity for individuals to make their own free choices?

    A. Agency

    B. Social control

    C. Structure

    D. Socialization

    E. Resocialization

74. A demographer would study all of the following topics EXCEPT:

    A. Fertility rates

    B. Infant mortality rates

    C. Migration patterns

    D. Reproductive rates

    E. Cultural meanings of in-vitro fertilization

75. In sociological models of social change, what both shapes and limits an individual's agency?

    A. Autonomy

    B. The social structure

    C. The looking glass self

    D. Deviance

    E. Impression management

76. **What is the term used to describe discrimination on the basis of age?**

    A. Heterosexism

    B. Prejudice

    C. Racism

    D. Ageism

    E. Sexism

77. **What is the primary vehicle for upward social mobility in the United States?**

    A. Winning the lottery

    B. Inheritance

    C. Education

    D. Hard work

    E. Marriage

78. **The term for norms, values, and beliefs that are conveyed indirectly in schools is:**

    A. Out of place policing

    B. Steering

    C. Institutional racism

    D. The hidden curriculum

    E. The school-to-prison pipeline

79. **Sociologists use the term _____ to describe a decline in the cultural and social significance of religion.**

    A. Atheism

    B. Anti-religious

    C. Modernization

    D. Secularization

    E. Rationalization

80. **Which sociological theory would argue that because some jobs are important to society, they should be more highly rewarded?**

    A. Structural Functionalism

    B. Rational Choice Theory

    C. Conflict Theory

    D. Racial Formation Theory

    E. Symbolic Interactionism

81. **What discredited theory maintains that poverty is perpetuated by the cultural deficiencies and behaviors of the poor?**

    A. Rational choice theory

    B. Culture of poverty theory

    C. Reproduction of poverty theory

    D. Conflict theory

    E. Racial formation theory

82. **A conflict theorist would make which of the following claims about deviance?**

    A. Deviance is functional for society

    B. Deviant behaviors only exist among the poor

    C. Deviant behavior is medicalized

    D. Deviant behaviors only exist among the rich

    E. Powerful groups label behaviors that do not benefit them as deviant

83. **The way that the federal poverty line is calculated is frequently criticized by sociologists because:**

    A. It is subject to interpretation

    B. It overestimates poverty in the U.S.

    C. It treats people as a number

    D. It excludes elder poverty

    E. It underestimates poverty because thresholds were developed in the 1960s and have not been revised to reflect rising costs of housing and healthcare

84. **What do sociologists call the process through which we learn what is appropriate for each gender?**

    A. Social Learning Theory

    B. Social structure

    C. Socialization

    D. Resocialization

    E. Social control

85. The study of aging is
_____.

A. Demography

B. Gerontology

C. Social structure

D. Socialization

E. Social control

86. What is the term given for social change that is initiated by individuals or groups with little or no formal institutional power?

A. Bottom-up social change

B. Top-down social change

C. Minion social change

D. Reactionary social change

E. Revolutionary social change

87. What term is used to describe a group of people who experienced the same event within the same time period?

A. Life course

B. Gerontology

C. Cohort

D. Elderly

E. Baby boomers

88. Residential communities that are within commuting distance to a larger city are known as
_____.

A. Rural areas

B. Exurbs

C. Urban areas

D. Suburbs

E. Gentrified cities

89. A population shift from rural to urban areas is called _____.

A. Gentrification

B. Urbanization

C. Suburbanization

D. Exurbanization

E. Urban renewal

90. What theory maintains that political power is distributed among many groups?

A. Pluralism

B. Marxism

C. Social Learning Theory

D. Rational Choice Theory

E. Multiple Group Theory

91. What is the term used in political sociology to describe legitimate or socially approved uses of power?

    A. Bureaucracy

    B. Social control

    C. Deviance

    D. Authority

    E. Rationality

92. What is the term used to describe a process whereby urban areas are revitalized?

    A. Urbanization

    B. Urban renewal

    C. Gentrification

    D. Suburbanization

    E. Exurbanization

93. Efforts to prevent or control deviant behavior is called _____.

    A. Social change

    B. Socialization

    C. Impression management

    D. Rationalization

    E. Social control

94. Which of the following statements about socialization is true?

    A. Socialization begins at birth

    B. Socialization begins when children enter kindergarten

    C. All cultures use the same socialization techniques

    D. Socialization stops in adolescence

    E. Resocialization is not possible

95. Who wrote that religion is the "opium of the people"?

    A. C. Wright Mills

    B. Karl Marx

    C. Max Weber

    D. Emile Durkheim

    E. Auguste Comte

96. **Which large-scale economic trend happened in the U.S. in the 1970s?**

    A. The number of manufacturing jobs increased

    B. The number of women in the workforce declined

    C. The number of the women in workforce increased

    D. Life expectancy declined

    E. Wages increased for the average worker

97. **Which of the following jobs would be considered part of the primary labor market?**

    A. A retail employee at a small boutique store

    B. A retail employee at a large discount store

    C. A bus driver

    D. An accountant

    E. A nanny

98. **Who believed that culture and ideas were the driving force of social change?**

    A. C. Wright Mills

    B. Karl Marx

    C. Max Weber

    D. Emile Durkheim

    E. Auguste Comte

99. **The primary source of strain in the typical one-parent household is:**

    A. The lack of a male role model

    B. Emotional stress caused by divorce

    C. That the children are being raised by only one parent

    D. Violence

    E. Poverty because most one-parent households are headed by women

100. **Examining the linkages between early and later life events is known as _____.**

    A. A life course approach

    B. Social Learning Theory

    C. An eco-cycle approach

    D. Resocialization

    E. Rational Choice theory

Answer Key

Question Number	Correct Answer	Your Answer	Question Number	Correct Answer	Your Answer	Question Number	Correct Answer	Your Answer
1	C		34	E		67	A	
2	A		35	A		68	C	
3	D		36	B		69	E	
4	E		37	D		70	D	
5	C		38	A		71	B	
6	B		39	C		72	E	
7	E		40	D		73	A	
8	D		41	B		74	E	
9	A		42	A		75	B	
10	B		43	C		76	D	
11	E		44	A		77	C	
12	A		45	D		78	D	
13	C		46	D		79	D	
14	D		47	B		80	A	
15	B		48	E		81	B	
16	C		49	A		82	E	
17	D		50	C		83	E	
18	A		51	B		84	C	
19	B		52	E		85	B	
20	E		53	C		86	A	
21	C		54	D		87	C	
22	B		55	A		88	D	
23	E		56	B		89	B	
24	A		57	C		90	A	
25	C		58	B		91	D	
26	D		59	D		92	B	
27	A		60	A		93	E	
28	E		61	E		94	A	
29	C		62	C		95	B	
30	C		63	E		96	C	
31	B		64	B		97	D	
32	D		65	C		98	C	
33	C		66	D		99	E	
						100	A	

RATIONALES

1. **Karl Marx is considered the founder of:**

    A. Structural Functionalism

    B. Rational Choice Theory

    C. Conflict Theory

    D. Racial Formation Theory

    E. Symbolic Interactionism

The answer is C.
C is correct. Karl Marx believed that all history was the result of class conflict. This idea is the basis for conflict theory which posits that society is characterized by conflict over resources between groups.

2. **A process where affluent people (often white) move into urban areas and displace the original lower-income residents (often people of color) is known as:**

    A. Gentrification

    B. Urban decay

    C. White flight

    D. Environmental racism

    E. Steering

The answer is A.
A is correct. Gentrification is when middle to upper-middle class people (often white) move into city cores, displacing poorer (often minority) populations.

3.   **The practice of placing students in higher and lower-level curriculum groups based on test scores, grades, and/ or teacher discretion is known as:**

A. The hidden curriculum

B. Accomplishment of natural growth

C. Stereotype threat

D. Tracking

E. The hidden threat

The answer is D.
D is correct. Tracking is when students are placed into different-level classes.

4.   **Sociologists often use samples to make inferences about a population. The most important quality of a sample is that it is:**

A. It is easy to conduct

B. It is inexpensive

C. It is large

D. It includes people who do not wish to participate

E. It is representative of the population

The answer is E.
E is correct. If your sample is not representative of the population it is drawn from, you cannot legitimately make inferences about the larger population. A, B, and C are nice characteristics to have but you cannot force people to participate in a research study (D).

5. **In the United States, it is usually considered rude not to make direct eye contact when talking to another person. Making eye contact is therefore an example of a:**

    A. Right

    B. Taboo

    C. Norm

    D. Value

    E. Law

The answer is C.
C is correct. Norms refer to socially acceptable ways of behaving.

6. **The process by which we learn how to become members of social and cultural groups is:**

    A. Learning

    B. Socialization

    C. Gendering

    D. Societization

    E. Culturalization

The answer is B.
B is correct. D and E are made up, A is too general, and C only refers to gender.

7.   **Failing to cover your mouth when you sneeze is a violation of a:**

   A. Taboo

   B. More

   C. Health code

   D. Law

   E. Folkway

The answer is E.
E is correct. Folkways are norms that guide casual interaction. Answer B, mores, are norms with greater moral significance. Taboos refer extreme prohibitions (e.g., taboos against incest). C and D are wrong because failure to cover your mouth when sneezing is not codified in laws or codes.

8.   **Sarah is a sociologist studying roller derbies. To collect data she joins a roller derby team. Sarah is conducting a(n):**

   A. Survey

   B. Experiment

   C. Content analysis

   D. Ethnography

   E. Natural experiment

The answer is D.
D is correct. An ethnography is a type of qualitative study whereby the researcher immerses himself or herself in a culture or context that he or she wants to study.

9.   The theory that views society as an organism in which all parts work together to promote stability is:

   A. Structural Functionalism

   B. Conflict Theory

   C. Symbolic Interactionism

   D. Structuralism

   E. Social Bonding Theory

The answer is A.
A is correct. Structural functionalism maintains that society is like an organism and each institution in society functions together so that society operates smoothly.

10.   Imagine you wanted to use the sociological imagination to understand depression. To do so, you might consider how an individual's likelihood of experiencing depression is related to:

   A. Personality

   B. Family income

   C. Use of anti-depressants

   D. Genetics

   E. Psychological history

The answer is B.
B is correct. The sociological imagination requires analyzing how personal issues/problems such as depression are related to larger social factors, like family income. All other answer choices refer to individual, personal characteristics, rather than social factors.

11. **When a group of people share a language, values, and a history they are referred to as a(n):**

   A. Racial group

   B. Subculture

   C. Family

   D. Tribe

   E. Ethnic group

The answer is E.
E is correct. An ethnic group refers to a group of people with a shared set of cultural characteristics. This is in contrast, for example, to race which is often presumed to have a biological basis.

12. **Social mobility happens most frequently in a:**

   A. Social class system

   B. Caste system

   C. Feudal system

   D. Slavery system

   E. Royal system

The answer is A.
A is correct. Social mobility is very rare or non-existent in the other systems listed (and royal system is not a sociological term).

13. **Which of the following is NOT a dimension of social class?**

    A. Wealth

    B. Income

    C. Race

    D. Educational Attainment

    E. Prestige

The answer is C.
C is correct. Wealth, income, educational attainment and prestige all dimensions of social class. Race is correlated with social class but it is a distinct construct.

14. **Which of the following is NOT an example of a social movement?**

    A. The Civil Rights Movement

    B. The Gay Rights Movement

    C. Feminism

    D. Roe v. Wade

    E. The Pro-Life Movement

The answer is D.
D is correct. Roe v. Wade is a piece of legislation, not a social movement.

15. **Women often do not reach the upper ranks of corporations due to an invisible barrier known as:**

    A. The glass escalator

    B. The glass ceiling

    C. Sexism

    D. Discrimination

    E. Racism

The answer is B.
B is correct. Answer A refers to a process where men in female-dominated occupations rise quickly through the ranks. Sexism and discrimination are too general. Racism explains why people of color are less likely to rise through the ranks of institutions.

16. **Most women in the United States take their husband's last name when they marry. This is evidence that the United States is:**

    A. Matrilineal

    B. Patrilineal

    C. Patriarchal

    D. Matriarchal

    E. Egalitarian

The answer is C.
C is correct. The reason The answer is not B is because patrilineal refers specifically to inheritance through male kin. For example, the fact that children usually inherit their father's last name would be an example of a patrilineal custom. In contrast, women take their husband's name not as a form of inheritance, but rather as a result of the greater power and prestige assigned to men in a patriarchal society.

17. **Which of the following terms refers to the belief that an individual's successes and failures in life are solely a result of effort, intelligence, and ability?**

    A. Stratification

    B. Class privilege

    C. Ideology

    D. The myth of meritocracy

    E. Color-blind racism

The answer is D.
D is correct. The myth of meritocracy refers to the erroneous belief system that how successful or unsuccessful a person is, particularly in terms of wealth, education, and status, is solely a reflection of merit or ability. This is erroneous from a sociological perspective because various social factors (e.g., family's income and educational attainment, gender, race, etc.) affect how successful and unsuccessful a person is. We know this is true because most people remain in the same social class as the family they were born into.

18. **"I am never asked to speak for all the people of my racial group" is an example of:**

    A. White privilege

    B. Class privilege

    C. Male privilege

    D. Structural inequality

    E. Color-blind racism

The answer is A.
A is correct. Whites in Western society have the privilege of not being asked to speak for all whites, unlike racial/ethnic minorities who are often asked questions such as "Well, what do other Black people think about ____."

19. **Who claimed that society is composed of two opposing social classes – the bourgeoisie and the proletariat?**

   A. C. Wright Mills

   B. Karl Marx

   C. Max Weber

   D. Emile Durkheim

   E. Auguste Comte

The answer is B.
B is correct. Karl Marx famously claimed that in modern capitalism society is composed of two opposing social classes – the bourgeoisie and the proletariat. See The Communist Manifesto.

20. **Who is considered the founder of sociology?**

   A. C. Wright Mills

   B. Karl Marx

   C. Max Weber

   D. Emile Durkheim

   E. Auguste Comte

The answer is E.
E is correct. Auguste Comte first used the word sociology and is considered to be the founder of the discipline.

21. **According to Emile Durkheim's famous study on suicide, suicide rates are higher among the unmarried compared to the married. Durkheim argued that this was became unmarried people _____.**

    A. Are less happy than married people

    B. Are less likely to be prevented from committing suicide by a spouse

    C. Have weaker social ties

    D. Are less likely to have access to mental health care

    E. Are more likely to be Protestant

The answer is C.
C is correct. The premise of Durkheim's famous multi-national study on suicide (published as the book, Suicide) is that groups with higher rates of social integration or stronger social ties (e.g., married people, people with children, Catholics) are less likely to commit suicide compared to people with lower rates of social integration or weaker social ties (e.g., the unmarried, the childless, Protestants).

22. **Teenagers who participate in abstinence-only sex education programs have higher rates of teen pregnancy than teenagers who do not participant in these programs. According to Merton, a famous structural-functionalist, this is an example of a(n)_____.**

    A. Manifest function

    B. Latent function

    C. Accidental function

    D. Structural function

    E. Unexpected function

The answer is B.
B is correct. According to Merton, latent functions are those that are neither intended nor recognized. In contrast, manifest functions (answer A) refer to the consequences that people observe or expect, those that are intended. C-E are not sociological concepts.

23. **Which of the following theories posits that individuals act in ways that are based on meanings formed through social interaction with others?**

    A. Structural Functionalism

    B. Rational Choice Theory

    C. Conflict Theory

    D. Racial Formation Theory

    E. Symbolic Interactionism

The answer is E.
E is correct. Symbolic interactionists posit that through social interaction we learn meanings about the social world and in turn, we replicate those meanings in social interaction. Thus, the basis for interaction is socially shared meanings.

24. **Ricardo tells a joke at a party and everyone stares blankly at him. He interprets their reactions to mean that he is not funny and in turn, worries that he is not a funny person. Ricardo's experience is an example of _____.**

    A. The looking glass self

    B. Differentiation of the self

    C. Embarrassment

    D. Imitating others

    E. Taking the role of the other

The answer is A.
A is correct. The looking glass self is a concept developed by Charles Horton Cooley to refer to a process whereby an individual 1) imagines how he or she appears to others, 2) imagines and reacts to what he or she feels others' judgment of that appearance is, and 3) develops a self based on those judgments.

25. **An Asian American woman with a college degree whose parents are doctors is likely to marry an Asian American man with a college degree and whose parents are professionals. This pattern is an example of _____.**

    A. Exogamy

    B. Monogamy

    C. Homogamy

    D. Patriarchy

    E. Propinquity

The answer is C.
C is correct. Homogamy refers to marriage between individuals who are similar in culturally important ways. In this case, this couple is homogamous in terms of family socioeconomic status, educational attainment, and race.

26. **Emile Durkheim developed a term to refer to a mismatch between personal standards and larger social standards. This term is _____.**

    A. Rebellion

    B. Socialization

    C. Group think

    D. Anomie

    E. Deviance

The answer is D.
D is correct. Anomie refers to the breakdown of social bonds between an individual and his or her community which results in situation of "normlessness." This breakdown is a result of a mismatch or incongruence between personal standards and larger social standards.

27. **When sociologists conduct experiments, they are attempting to isolate and measure the effect produced by a(n) _____.**

    A. Independent variable

    B. Dependent variable

    C. Confounding variable

    D. Mediating variable

    E. Moderating variable

The answer is A.
A is correct. Experiments are conducted in order to isolate and measure the effect of an independent variable (e.g., the presence of an authority figure) on a dependent variable (e.g., if individuals will shock respondents who answer questions incorrectly – see the Milgram experiment).

28. **A positive correlation or association refers to when _____.**

    A. Variables stay the same

    B. Something good happens

    C. One variable goes up and another goes down

    D. Two variables move in opposite directions

    E. Two variables move in the same direction

The answer is E.
E is correct. For example, there is a positive correlation between income and educational attainment; on average people who have higher levels of income also have higher levels of educational attainment while the reverse is true as well -- people who have lower levels of income also tend to have lower levels of educational attainment.

29. **Rowan examined advertisements in magazines in order to understand the different ways that men and women are portrayed in advertisements. This is an example of a(n) _____.**

    A. Survey

    B. Experiment

    C. Content analysis

    D. Ethnography

    E. Natural experiment

The answer is C.
C is correct. Content analysis is a method of examining written, oral, visual, or audio-visual media that is used in sociology to make inferences about the social world. It can be quantitative or qualitative.

30. **After the passage of Brown v. Board of Education of Topeka, there was a mass exodus of whites from racially-diverse urban areas to racially-homogenous suburbs. This process is: _____.**

    A. Gentrification

    B. Urban decay

    C. White flight

    D. Environmental racism

    E. Steering

The answer is C.
C is correct. White flight refers to when whites flee racially-diverse communities for more racially-homogenous communities. The most cited example of this is when in the 1950s and 1960s large numbers of whites left racially-diverse urban areas for racially-homogenous suburban areas. Some sociologists posit this happened because whites did not want their children to attend integrated schools in urban areas.

31. **Rates of poverty in the United States are highest for which of the following groups?**

   A. The elderly

   B. Children under 18

   C. Unmarried men

   D. Married couple households

   E. Individuals who live in urban areas

The answer is B.
B is correct. As of the 2010 census, 22% of American children are poor and the U.S. has the highest rate of childhood poverty of all developed nations. This is higher than the rates for the other groups listed here.

32. **The fact that environmentally hazardous materials (e.g., toxic waste, pollution) are more likely to be located in low-income or minority communities is referred to as _____.**

   A. Gentrification

   B. Urban decay

   C. White flight

   D. Environmental racism

   E. Environmental injustice

The answer is D.
D is correct. Environmental racism refers to the fact that environmentally hazardous materials are more likely to be located in communities with a high percentage of racial/ethnic minorities and low-income individuals. This is because these groups have less political, economic, and social clout that more affluent groups.

33. **The fact that, on average, non-white children go to schools with fewer resources compared to white children is an example of _____.**

    A. Overt racism

    B. Covert racism

    C. Institutional racism

    D. Prejudice

    E. Segregation

The answer is C.
C is correct. Institutional racism refers to when racism is built into the structure of institutions. Contrary to common belief in American society, most racial/ethnic inequality is not perpetuated by individuals being overtly or covertly racist. Rather, it is perpetuated by institutional racism whereby social institutions are structured in such a way that systematically benefit whites and systematically disadvantage people of color.

34. **Which group has the lowest marriage rates in the United States?**

    A. White men

    B. Black men

    C. Hispanic men

    D. Hispanic women

    E. Black women

The answer is E.
E is correct. Black women have the lowest marriage rates of all racial/gender groups.

35. **According to Merton's strain theory, which type of deviance occurs when an individual accepts cultural goals (e.g., getting rich) but rejects the socially acceptable means of achieving them (e.g., by stealing)?**

    A. Innovation

    B. Conformity

    C. Ritualism

    D. Retreatism

    E. Rebellion

The answer is A.
A is correct. In Merton's strain theory, innovation refers to an acceptance of cultural goals but a rejection of socially acceptable means to achieve them. Therefore, if you accepted the cultural goal of being wealthy but had to steal to attain this goal you would be rejecting socially accepted means to achieve wealth (e.g., work hard).

36. **Sociologists believe that sex is _____whereas gender is _____.**

    A. Socially constructed; biological

    B. Biological; socially constructed

    C. Relevant; irrelevant

    D. Irrelevant; relevant

    E. Mutable; immutable

The answer is B.
B is correct. Sex is usually considered a biological trait, whereas gender is learned through socialization and therefore is socially constructed or based on socially shared meaning systems (which are not necessarily grounded in biological differences).

37. **Over the past several decades, the U.S. economy has shifted from one based on _____ to one based on _____.**

    A. Services; manufacturing

    B. Manufacturing; goods

    C. Goods; manufacturing

    D. Manufacturing; services

    E. Finances; goods

The answer is D.
D is correct. The U.S. economy has radically transformed from one based on the manufacturing of goods to one based on the production of services. Beginning on a large scale in the 1970s, manufacturing companies have left the United States, in search of cheaper labor overseas.

38. **Which of the following statements about social mobility in the U.S. is false?**

    A. Anyone who works hard enough will achieve upward mobility

    B. Most social mobility happens within the middle class (e.g., from lower middle class to upper middle class)

    C. Most people remain in the same social class as their family of origin

    D. Educational attainment matters for social mobility

    E. Social mobility is usually related to societal-level factors, not individual ones

The answer is A.
A is correct. Despite popular perception, not everyone who works hard will achieve upward mobility. Many working poor people in this country work long hours but fail to escape poverty.

39. **If a new employee starts working at a faster pace than the other workers, this an example of _____.**

    A. Efficiency

    B. Division of labor

    C. Rate busting

    D. Loafing

    E. Rate setting

The answer is C.
C is correct. Rate busting is a labor term that emerged from the study of manufacturing jobs. In order to avoid a reduction in the piece rate of manufactured products, factory workers usually agree on a rate at which to produce products. Breaking this agreement is known as rate busting.

40. **We are just beginning to witness which of the following large-scale demographic shifts?**

    A. An increase in the divorce rate

    B. An increase in age at first marriage

    C. An increase in age at first birth

    D. An increase in the percentage of the population that is 65 and older

    E. An increase in stay-at-home mothers

The answer is D.
D is correct. Beginning in 2011, the baby boomers started turning 65. Because the baby boomers are a very large generation, the U.S. has started to witness a dramatic increase in the percentage of the population that is over 65.

41. **Which of the following demographic trends did NOT occur in the 20ᵗʰ century?**

A. An increase in life expectancy

B. Migration from urban to rural areas

C. An increase in female-headed households

D. An increase in the divorce rate

E. An increase in the number of women in the labor force

The answer is B.
B is correct. The opposite took place; the 20th century was characterized by a large-scale rural to urban migration and the growth of cities.

42. **Urban ethnographic sociology emerged from:**

A. The Chicago school

B. The New York school

C. The Harvard school

D. The Emory school

E. The Yale school

The answer is A.
A is correct. The Chicago School is the birth of urban ethnography.

43. **Which famous sociologist argued that capitalism was a result of the Protestant ethic?**

A. C. Wright Mills

B. Karl Marx

C. Max Weber

D. Emile Durkheim

E. Auguste Comte

The answer is C.
C is correct. Max Weber argued that capitalism emerged from Protestant, particularly, Calvinist, beliefs. See The Protestant Ethic and the Spirit of Capitalism.

44. **Which famous sociologist wrote about the power elite?**

A. C. Wright Mills

B. Karl Marx

C. Max Weber

D. Emile Durkheim

E. Auguste Comte

The answer is A.
A is correct. C. Wright Mills argued that society is run by a power elite who control the economy, political system, and military. See The Power Elite.

45. **Which famous sociologist is considered the first academic sociologist?**

    A. C. Wright Mills

    B. Karl Marx

    C. Max Weber

    D. Emile Durkheim

    E. Auguste Comte

The answer is D.
D is correct. Emile Durkheim is considered the first academic sociologist because he institutionalized sociology when he founded the first French department of sociology in 1895.

46. **Food deserts refer to:**

    A. Desert communities where there is too much food

    B. Desert communities with unhealthy foods

    C. Desert communities with not enough food

    D. Communities that lack access to fresh, healthy foods

    E. Communities without any restaurants

The answer is D.
D is correct. Food deserts are communities that lack access to fresh, healthy foods. These are usually located in low-income, minority, urban neighborhoods. While these communities do not lack access to food, per se, most of the food available consists of fast food or packaged foods with high levels of preservatives, sugar, and fat.

47. Which sociological theory maintains that reality is based on culturally agreed upon meanings?

    A. Rational choice theory

    B. Social constructionism

    C. Positivism

    D. Structural functionalism

    E. Conflict theory

The answer is B.
B is correct. A social constructionist perspective maintains that reality is a product of culturally agreed upon meanings. For example, social constructionists argue that racial differences are socially constructed rather than biological facts. This is because genetic differences do not fit neatly into the racial categories that society has created.

48. Which statement best describes trends in the economy since the 1970s?

    A. Declining levels of income inequality

    B. Declining levels of wealth inequality

    C. Declining levels of income and wealth inequality

    D. Increasing levels of income inequality

    E. Increasing levels of income and wealth inequality

The answer is E.
E is correct. The U.S. economy has been categorized by widening levels of income and wealth inequality since the 1970s.

49. **What is the term used to describe a process by which human conditions become defined and treated as medical conditions?**

    A. Medicalization

    B. Mentalization

    C. Healthism

    D. Pathologism

    E. Deviation

The answer is A.
A is correct. Medicalization refers to turning various human conditions into medical problems. For example, impotence (previously considered a fact of life) has been transformed into "erectile dysfunction," which requires medical intervention.

50. **Which famous sociologist wrote extensively about bureaucracy?**

    A. C. Wright Mills

    B. Karl Marx

    C. Max Weber

    D. Emile Durkheim

    E. Auguste Comte

The answer is C.
C is correct. Max Weber wrote extensively about bureaucracy, particularly in his famous book, Economy and Society.

51. **The McDonaldization of society refers to:**

    A. The spread of McDonald's chains all over the globe

    B. A process by which cultural products become homogenous and predictable

    C. An increase in the number of fast food restaurants

    D. The rise in obesity rates

    E. The rise in the number of foods with preservatives

The answer is B.
B is correct. George Ritzer coined the term the McDonaldization of society to refer to a process whereby all sorts of cultural products become homogenous and predictable. For example, a hamburger is the same in California and New York. Similarly, when consumers enter numerous other chain stores, products are homogenous and predictable.

52. **Research that uses both qualitative and quantitative methods is known as:**

    A. Ethnography

    B. Participant observation

    C. Action research

    D. Experiments

    E. Mixed methods

The answer is E.
E is correct. Mixed methods is the term for research that uses both qualitative and quantitative methods.

53. **Quantitative methods are best for:**

A. Exploratory research

B. Collecting non-numerical data

C. Confirming a hypothesis

D. Generating a new theory

E. Small sample sizes

The answer is C.
C is correct. Quantitative methods are best suited for testing a hypothesis with statistical analyses. All the other answer choices better characterize qualitative methods.

54. **Research that attempts to understand the past is referred to as:**

A. Experimental

B. Survey research

C. Ethnography

D. Historical research

E. Mixed methods

The answer is D.
D is correct. Historical research examines a research question about the past.

55. **Brianna moves from a small rural town in Pennsylvania to New York City. She is overwhelmed by the fast pace of life in New York. The term that best describes her experience is _____.**

    A. Culture shock

    B. Socialization

    C. The looking glass self

    D. Deviance

    E. Social control

The answer is A
A is correct. Culture shock is disorientation based on experiencing a new culture or way of life.

56. **Which of the following is an example of a counterculture?**

    A. Catholics

    B. The Amish

    C. Nurses

    D. Athletes

    E. Latinos

The answer is B.
B is correct. The Amish are a counterculture because their values and way of living are opposed to mainstream American values and ways of living.

57. **Which of the following is an example of an occupation in the secondary labor market?**

    A. Physician

    B. Professor

    C. Fast food worker

    D. Lawyer

    E. Plumber

The answer is C.
C is correct. Fast food workers are part of the secondary labor market because the secondary labor market is composed of jobs that are usually part-time or temporary and have high turnover and low pay.

58. **Which of the following statements about stratification is true?**

    A. All societies have equal levels of stratification

    B. All societies have some form of stratification

    C. Capitalist societies have less inequality than socialist ones

    D. Levels of stratification have not changed over time in the U.S.

    E. Social mobility is not possible in class-based societies

The answer is B.
B is correct. All societies have some form of stratification.

59. **Behaviors that violate social norms are referred to as _____.**

   A. Culture shock

   B. Socialization

   C. The looking glass self

   D. Deviance

   E. Social control

The answer is D.
D is correct. Deviant behaviors are behaviors that violate social norms.

60. **Which institution is primarily responsible for reproducing members of society?**

   A. The family

   B. The economy

   C. Religion

   D. Education

   E. Politics

The answer is A.
A is correct. One important function of the family is to reproduce members of society.

61. **What explanation does NOT explain why women are paid less than men?**

     A. Discrimination

     B. Men and women tend to have different occupations

     C. Men and women tend to have different specialties within occupations

     D. Women have primarily responsibility for childcare

     E. Women are less concerned with income

The answer is E.
E is correct. It is not true that women are less concerned with income. All other answers help to explain the gender pay gap.

62. **The practice of women taking two or more husbands at a time is known as:**

     A. Monogamy

     B. Polygyny

     C. Polyandry

     D. Bigamy

     E. Bisexuality

The answer is C.
C is correct. Polyandry is the term used to describe the practice of having two or more husbands at a time.

63. **Policies and practices that push schoolchildren (particularly low-income minorities) out of classrooms and into the criminal justice systems is referred to as:**

    A. Out of place policing

    B. Steering

    C. Institutional racism

    D. The hidden curriculum

    E. The school-to-prison pipeline

The answer is E.
E is correct. The school-to-prison pipeline refers to a wide variety of policies and practices (e.g., zero-tolerance policies; high stakes testing) that directly and indirectly push students (often low-income, minority boys) out of schools and into the juvenile justice system.

64. **Schools in the U.S. have dramatically different levels of resources, in part, because school funding at the local level comes primarily from:**

    A. Income taxes

    B. Property taxes

    C. Sales taxes

    D. Donations

    E. Tax credits

The answer is B.
B is correct. Property taxes form the primary base of school funding at the local level. And because wealthier people tend to have more expensive homes and higher property taxes, wealthier children tend to go to schools with more resources.

65. **Which group is NOT under-represented in the U.S. Congress?**

    A. Women

    B. Latinos

    C. Whites

    D. African Americans

    E. Asian Americans

The answer is C.
C is correct. Whites are over-represented in Congress, meaning there are a higher percentage of whites in Congress than we would expect based on the racial/ethnic make-up of the U.S. population. All other groups listed here are under-represented, meaning there are a lower percentage of these groups in Congress than we would expect based on the gender and racial/ethnic make-up of the U.S. population.

66. **The process by which existing social roles and norms are altered or replaced by new ones is known as:**

    A. Culture shock

    B. Socialization

    C. The looking glass self

    D. Resocialization

    E. Social control

The answer is D.
D is correct. Resocialization is the process of learning new social norms and roles.

67. **A type of social movement that advocates for the restoration of a previous social arrangement (e.g., for the repeal of Roe v. Wade) is known as a _____ social movement.**

    A. Reactionary

    B. Reformist

    C. Revolutionary

    D. Personal transformation

    E. Civil Rights

The answer is A.
A is correct. Reactionary social movements are social movements that advocate for the restoration of a previous state of social affairs. In this case, the pro-life movement which advocates for the repeal of Roe v. Wade is an example of a reactionary social movement.

68. **A process by which collective delusions of threats to society spread rapidly through a social group is known as _____.**

    A. Social control

    B. Deviance

    C. Mass hysteria

    D. The bystander effect

    E. The looking glass self

The answer is C.
C is correct. Mass hysteria is when a group of people all suffer from a collective delusion. An example of mass hysteria is the panicked reaction to the radio broadcasting of The War of the Worlds.

69. **A process by which individuals attempt to influence the perceptions of others is referred to as _____.**

    A. Social control

    B. Deviance

    C. The bystander effect

    D. The looking glass self

    E. Impression management

The answer is E.
E is correct. See Erving Goffman's The Presentation of Self in Everyday Life.

70. **The process by which individuals do not offer assistance to victims when other people are present is referred to as _____.**

    A. Social control

    B. Deviance

    C. Mass hysteria

    D. The bystander effect

    E. The looking glass self

The answer is D.
D is correct. See the case of Kitty Genovese for an example.

71. **The Hispanic paradox is the name given to describe the fact that despite having lower average incomes than whites, Hispanics in the U.S. have _____ compared to whites.**

    A. Higher levels of educational attainment

    B. Better health outcomes

    C. Larger families

    D. Higher marriage rates

    E. Fewer children

The answer is B.
B is correct. The Hispanic Paradox is an epidemiological paradox whereby despite having lower average incomes than whites, Hispanics in the U.S. have better health outcomes than whites on a number of measures, including life expectancy. This is a paradox because income is positively correlated with better health outcomes. Why this paradox is the case is not known, although some theories include the fact that Hispanics have higher levels of social integration and first-generation immigrants are healthier than native-born Americans.

72. **A medical sociologist would study all of the following topics EXCEPT:**

    A. Mortality patterns

    B. Marriage and health

    C. Erectile dysfunction

    D. Cesarean sections

    E. Political candidates

The answer is E.
E is correct. Medical sociologists would not study political candidates. Political sociologists would.

73. **Which of the following sociological terms refers to the capacity for individuals to make their own free choices?**

    A. Agency

    B. Social control

    C. Structure

    D. Socialization

    E. Resocialization

The answer is A.
A is correct. Agency is the capacity to make free choices. A key debate in sociology is the role of agency versus structure.

74. **A demographer would study all of the following topics EXCEPT:**

    A. Fertility rates

    B. Infant mortality rates

    C. Migration patterns

    D. Reproductive rates

    E. Cultural meanings of in-vitro fertilization

The answer is E.
E is correct. Qualitative sociologists, not demographers, would study the meanings of something (e.g., in vitro fertilization). Traditionally, demographers have studied fertility/reproductive rates, migration, and mortality.

75. **In sociological models of social change, what both shapes and limits an individual's agency?**

    A. Autonomy

    B. The social structure

    C. The looking glass self

    D. Deviance

    E. Impression management

The answer is B
B is correct. Sociologists believe that social structures both shape and limit individuals' agency. See agency versus structure debate in sociology.

76. **What is the term used to describe discrimination on the basis of age?**

    A. Heterosexism

    B. Prejudice

    C. Racism

    D. Ageism

    E. Sexism

The answer is D.
D is correct. Ageism is the term used to describe discrimination on the basis of age.

77. **What is the primary vehicle for upward social mobility in the United States?**

    A. Winning the lottery

    B. Inheritance

    C. Education

    D. Hard work

    E. Marriage

The answer is C.
C is correct. Education is the primary vehicle for upward mobility in the United States.

78. **The term for norms, values, and beliefs that are conveyed indirectly in schools is:**

    A. Out of place policing

    B. Steering

    C. Institutional racism

    D. The hidden curriculum

    E. The school-to-prison pipeline

The answer is D.
D is correct. The hidden curriculum refers to messages that are conveyed indirectly in schools. For example, the fact that teachers often label black boys "bad" or "troublemakers" indirectly sends the message that black boys are deviant or criminal (see A.A. Ferguson's Bad Boys: Public Schools and the Making of Black Masculinity).

79. Sociologists use the term _____ to describe a decline in the cultural and social significance of religion.

    A. Atheism

    B. Anti-religious

    C. Modernization

    D. Secularization

    E. Rationalization

The answer is D.
D is correct. Secularization is used to describe the decline in the cultural and social significance of religion.

80. Which sociological theory would argue that because some jobs are important to society, they should be more highly rewarded?

    A. Structural Functionalism

    B. Rational Choice Theory

    C. Conflict Theory

    D. Racial Formation Theory

    E. Symbolic Interactionism

The answer is A.
A is correct. Structural functionalists maintain that most existing structural arrangements are functional for society. Therefore, the fact that some jobs are more highly rewarded is considered functional in that it motivates people to work hard and attain high levels of education.

81. **What discredited theory maintains that poverty is perpetuated by the cultural deficiencies and behaviors of the poor?**

    A. Rational choice theory

    B. Culture of poverty theory

    C. Reproduction of poverty theory

    D. Conflict theory

    E. Racial formation theory

The answer is B.
B is correct. The culture of poverty theory is a discredited theory that maintains that cultural aspects of the poor (e.g., that the poor are lazy and unable to delay gratification) keep them in a cycle of poverty. Although most sociologists believe that poverty is a result of various structural factors, U.S. welfare policy has been informed by a culture of poverty theory in that it requires that recipients work or receive work training based on the belief that a failure to value work is why recipients are poor.

82. **A conflict theorist would make which of the following claims about deviance?**

    A. Deviance is functional for society

    B. Deviant behaviors only exist among the poor

    C. Deviant behavior is medicalized

    D. Deviant behaviors only exist among the rich

    E. Powerful groups label behaviors that do not benefit them as deviant

The answer is E.
E is correct. Conflict theorists believe that economically and politically powerful groups are able to define reality for all. Thus, powerful groups can label behaviors that do not benefit them and their interests as deviant. See the concept of ideology and Karl Marx.

83. **The way that the federal poverty line is calculated is frequently criticized by sociologists because:**

    A. It is subject to interpretation

    B. It overestimates poverty in the U.S.

    C. It treats people as a number

    D. It excludes elder poverty

    E. It underestimates poverty because thresholds were developed in the 1960s and have not been revised to reflect rising costs of housing and healthcare

The answer is E.
E is correct. Poverty thresholds are considered outdated because they are based on the assumption that 1/3rd of a family's income is spent on food. However, most families today spend much less than 1/3rd of their income on food, due to rising costs of healthcare and housing. More accurately, most families spend about 1/5th of their income on food, in which case the poverty threshold should be five times the cost of food for a given family size and would include many more people.

84. **What do sociologists call the process through which we learn what is appropriate for each gender?**

    A. Social Learning Theory

    B. Social structure

    C. Socialization

    D. Resocialization

    E. Social control

The answer is C.
C is correct. We learn what is appropriate for boys and girls through the process of socialization.

85. **The study of aging is _____.**

    A. Demography

    B. Gerontology

    C. Social structure

    D. Socialization

    E. Social control

The answer is B.
B is correct. Gerontology is the study of aging.

86. **What is the term given for social change that is initiated by individuals or groups with little or no formal institutional power?**

    A. Bottom-up social change

    B. Top-down social change

    C. Minion social change

    D. Reactionary social change

    E. Revolutionary social change

The answer is A.
A is correct. Bottom-up social change is social change that originates from the bottom (i.e., from people with little institutional power). Grassroots social movements are examples of this type of social change.

87. **What term is used to describe a group of people who experienced the same event within the same time period?**

    A. Life course

    B. Gerontology

    C. Cohort

    D. Elderly

    E. Baby boomers

The answer is C.
C is correct. For example, a birth cohort refers to a group of people who were born in a certain time interval and therefore experienced certain life events together (e.g., baby boomers are a birth cohort who experienced Vietnam in their youth).

88. **Residential communities that are within commuting distance to a larger city are known as _____.**

    A. Rural areas

    B. Exurbs

    C. Urban areas

    D. Suburbs

    E. Gentrified cities

The answer is D.
D is correct. Suburbs are residential communities in commuting distance to a larger urban area.

89. **A population shift from rural to urban areas is called _____.**

    A. Gentrification

    B. Urbanization

    C. Suburbanization

    D. Exurbanization

    E. Urban renewal

The answer is B.
B is correct. Urbanization refers to the movement of people from rural to urban areas and the development of large cities.

90. **What theory maintains that political power is distributed among many groups?**

    A. Pluralism

    B. Marxism

    C. Social Learning Theory

    D. Rational Choice Theory

    E. Multiple Group Theory

The answer is A.
A is correct. Political pluralism is the belief that power and is (and should be) distributed among several political groups.

91. **What is the term used in political sociology to describe legitimate or socially approved uses of power?**

   A. Bureaucracy

   B. Social control

   C. Deviance

   D. Authority

   E. Rationality

The answer is D.
D is correct. Authority is the power or right to command or control, based on social legitimacy.

92. **What is the term used to describe a process whereby urban areas are revitalized?**

   A. Urbanization

   B. Urban renewal

   C. Gentrification

   D. Suburbanization

   E. Exurbanization

The answer is B.
B is correct. Urban renewal refers to land redevelopment in urban areas that had previously been in decay. Urban renewal often occurs simultaneously with gentrification.

93. **Efforts to prevent or control deviant behavior is called _____.**

A. Social change

B. Socialization

C. Impression management

D. Rationalization

E. Social control

The answer is E.
E is correct. Social control efforts attempt to prevent or control deviant behavior.

94. **Which of the following statements about socialization is true?**

A. Socialization begins at birth

B. Socialization begins when children enter kindergarten

C. All cultures use the same socialization techniques

D. Socialization stops in adolescence

E. Resocialization is not possible

The answer is A.
A. is correct. Socialization begins at birth and is typically a life-long process.

95. **Who wrote that religion is the "opium of the people"?**

    A. C. Wright Mills

    B. Karl Marx

    C. Max Weber

    D. Emile Durkheim

    E. Auguste Comte

The answer is B.
B is correct. Karl Marx wrote about religion as the "opium of the people," which is often paraphrased as "opiate of the masses." See Marx's Critique of Hegel's Philosophy of Right.

96. **Which large-scale economic trend happened in the U.S. in the 1970s?**

    A. The number of manufacturing jobs increased

    B. The number of women in the workforce declined

    C. The number of the women in workforce increased

    D. Life expectancy declined

    E. Wages increased for the average worker

The answer is C.
C is correct. The number of women in the workforce increased dramatically in the 1970s as a result of men's wages stagnating. All the other trends listed here did not occur.

97. **Which of the following jobs would be considered part of the primary labor market?**

    A. A retail employee at a small boutique store

    B. A retail employee at a large discount store

    C. A bus driver

    D. An accountant

    E. A nanny

The answer is D.
D is correct. Primary labor market jobs generally consist of high-wage jobs with benefits, security, and a career ladder. They often also require formal education, although not always because many skilled trade jobs (e.g., plumbers, electrician) do not always require formal education.

98. **Who believed that culture and ideas were the driving force of social change?**

    A. C. Wright Mills

    B. Karl Marx

    C. Max Weber

    D. Emile Durkheim

    E. Auguste Comte

The answer is C.
C is correct. Weber's belief in the importance of culture and ideas is evident in his famous book, The Protestant Ethic and the Spirit of Capitalism. In this book he argues that the development of capitalism was a direct result of Protestant beliefs, most specifically Calvinist beliefs about hard work and the notion of being (monetarily) rewarded on earth as a sign of salvation.

99. **The primary source of strain in the typical one-parent household is:**

A. The lack of a male role model

B. Emotional stress caused by divorce

C. That the children are being raised by only one parent

D. Violence

E. Poverty because most one-parent households are headed by women

The answer is E.
E is correct. Most single parent households are headed by women and these households are the most likely to be poor.

100. **Examining the linkages between early and later life events is known as _____.**

A. A life course approach

B. Social Learning Theory

C. An eco-cycle approach

D. Resocialization

E. Rational Choice theory

The answer is A.
A is correct. A life course approach, which is common in the sociology of aging, examines how early life experiences are linked to later life experiences.

Description of the Examination
The Social Sciences and History examination covers a wide range of topics from the social sciences and history disciplines. While the exam is based on no specific course, its content is drawn from introductory college courses that cover United States history, Western civilization, world history, government/political science, geography, sociology, economics, psychology, and anthropology.

The primary objective of the exam is to give candidates the opportunity to demonstrate that they possess the level of knowledge and understanding expected of college students who meet a distribution or general education requirement in the social sciences/history areas.

The Social Sciences and History examination contains approximately 120 questions to be answered in 90 minutes. Some of them are pretest questions that will not be scored. Any time candidates spend on tutorials and providing personal information is in addition to the actual testing time.

Note: This examination uses the chronological designations b.c.e. (before the common era) and c.e. (common era). These labels correspond to b.c. (before Christ) and a.d. (anno Domini), which are used in some textbooks.

Knowledge and Skills Required
The Social Sciences and History examination requires candidates to demonstrate one or more of the following abilities.
- Familiarity with terminology, facts, conventions, methodology, concepts, principles, generalizations, and theories
- Ability to understand, interpret, and analyze graphic, pictorial, and written material

- Ability to apply abstractions to particulars and to apply hypotheses, concepts, theories, and principles to given data

The content of the exam is drawn from the following disciplines. The percentages next to the main disciplines indicate the approximate percentage of exam questions on that topic.

40%   **History**
Requires general knowledge and understanding of time- and place-specific human experiences. Topics covered include political, diplomatic, social, economic, intellectual, and cultural material.

17%   **United States History**
Covers the colonial period, the American Revolution, the early republic, the Civil War and Reconstruction, industrialization, the Progressive Era, the First World War, the 1920s, the Great Depression and the New Deal, the Second World War, the 1950s, the Cold War, social conflict-the 1960s and 1970s, the late twentieth century

15%   **Western Civilization**
Covers ancient Western Asia, Egypt, Greece, and Rome as well as medieval Europe and modern Europe, including its expansion and outposts in other parts of the world

8%   **World History**
Covers Africa, Asia, Australia, Europe, North America, and South America from prehistory to the present, including global themes and interactions

13% **Government/Political Science**
- Comparative politics
- International relations
- Methods
- United States institutions
- Voting and political behaviour

11% **Geography**
- Cartographic methods
- Cultural geography
- Physical geography
- Population
- Regional geography
- Spatial interaction

10% **Economics**
- Economic measurements
- International trade
- Major theorists and schools
- Monetary and fiscal policy
- Product markets
- Resource markets
- Scarcity, choice, and cost

10% **Psychology**
- Aggression
- Biopsychology
- Conformity
- Group process
- Major theorists and schools
- Methods
- Performance
- Personality
- Socialization

10% **Sociology**
- Demography
- Deviance
- Family
- Interaction
- Major theorists and schools
- Methods
- Social change
- Social organization
- Social stratification
- Social theory

6% **Anthropology**
- Cultural anthropology
- Ethnography
- Major theorists and schools
- Methods
- Paleoanthropology

SAMPLE TEST

DIRECTIONS: Read each item and select the best response.

1. The _____ Incident occurred in August 1964, when two US destroyers were allegedly torpedoed by North Vietnamese, which led to American assistance in South Vietnam – although many claimed, and still maintain, that this was a "false flag" operation.

    A. Ho Chi Minh

    B. Straits of Malacca

    C. Mekong River

    D. Tet Offensive

    E. Gulf of Tonkin

2. What did opponents in America call the purchase of Alaska from the Russians in 1867, named after the contemporary Republican Party Secretary of State that orchestrated the move?

    A. Putyatin's Madness

    B. Johnson's Fault

    C. Seward's Folly

    D. Sitka's Scandal

    E. Barker's Blunder

3. Which nation did the United States fight against in the War of 1812?

    A. The United Kingdom

    B. Cuba

    C. Japan

    D. Russia

    E. France

4. Which of the following foreign policies accurately represents the 1947 Truman Doctrine?

    A. Providing aid to any country that wanted to rollback its political system

    B. Providing aid to the Midwest to improve their healthcare

    C. Providing aid to Southeast Asian nations so they could compete with India

    D. Providing aid to European countries because they were poor

    E. Providing aid to democratic countries to contain the spread of communism

5. **In May 1790, Rhode Island became the final state to ratify which of the following documents?**

    A. Homestead Act

    B. Constitution of the United States

    C. Civil Rights Act

    D. Emancipation Proclamation

    E. Declaration of Independence

6. **As a result of United States intervention in the Cuban War of Independence (1895-1898), which of the following countries did the United States declare war on in 1898?**

    A. Canada

    B. Russia

    C. France

    D. Spain

    E. The United Kingdom

7. **What event are the Sons of Liberty best known for undertaking?**

    A. The assassination of Archduke Franz Ferdinand of Austria, 1914

    B. The Massacre of Wounded Knee, 1890

    C. The Pueblo Revolt, 1680

    D. The River Run Riot, 2002

    E. The Boston Tea Party, 1773

8. **What was the major result of the American victory against Japan in the Battle of Leyte Gulf, Philippines, in 1944?**

    A. The Japanese retaliated by striking at the American fleet stationed at Pearl Harbour

    B. The Japanese fleet was effectively destroyed, causing them to abandon their occupation of Southeast Asia and crippling their Pacific naval force

    C. The Japanese army decided that Indonesia and Borneo were easier targets, and invaded them the following year in their 'Dutch East Indies campaign'

    D. The Philippines were then divided between America and Japan, allowing each country to exploit resources found in the archipelago

    E. The Japanese fleet escaped to their naval bases to refuel before returning in even greater numbers in 1946

9. **What does "virtual representation" mean, in the context of the American War of Independence?**

   A. Members of British Parliament claimed to have to the right to speak for and manage the affairs of all British subjects around the world

   B. The claiming of federal land grants by ex-slaves aged 21 years or over

   C. Native American tribes campaigned for their own representatives in the United States government

   D. The United States leadership provided grants of land for third-level educational institutes to train the next generation of politicians

   E. Citizens of the United States wanted the right to vote over the internet and by post

10. **Which U.S. president ordered the invasion of the Bay of Pigs, and in which year?**

    A. Lyndon B. Johnson, 1964

    B. Harry S. Truman, 1962

    C. John F. Kennedy, 1961

    D. Dwight D. Eisenhower, 1960

    E. Richard M. Nixon, 1963

11. **Which event eventually led to the resignation of President Richard Nixon?**

    A. The Florida State Voting Recount

    B. The Chappaquiddick Incident

    C. The Watergate Scandal

    D. The Lewinsky Affair

    E. Abu Ghraib prison abuse

12. **Which Native American tribe separated from the Shoshone after the Pueblo Revolt (1680), and were famous for their prowess on horseback? They occupied the southwest Great Plains, and today mainly reside in Oklahoma, Texas and New Mexico.**

    A. Apache

    B. Wampanoag

    C. Ojibwe

    D. Comanche

    E. Sioux

13. **Following the Indian Removal Act (1830), a number of Native American nations were forcibly relocated from their ancestral homelands in the American Southeast to "Indian Territory" west of the Mississippi. By what name is this event known as?**

    A. The Quetta Annexation

    B. The Trail of Tears

    C. The Expulsion of the Moriscos

    D. The Highland Clearances

    E. The Santiago de Compostela

14. **What did the Thirteenth Amendment to the Constitution, passed in December 1865, accomplish?**

    A. Abolition of slavery, except as punishment for a crime

    B. Protected the right to keep and bear arms

    C. The right to be secure against unreasonable searches and seizures

    D. Began electing US Senators by popular vote

    E. Provided the right to trial by jury

15. **Which of the following occurred between 1800 and 1900?**

    A. George Washington died

    B. New Mexico became the 47th US state

    C. Native Americans given the right to vote

    D. The Wall Street Crash

    E. The *Cross of Gold* speech was delivered by William Jennings Bryan

16. **What was the "Dust Bowl", which had a phenomenal influence on the severity of the Great Depression?**

    A. An act passed which raised import duties for alcohol, causing widespread protests by those in need of drink

    B. A giant curved dam was built at Grand Rapids, Michigan, which caused major rivers to dry up and the water table to sink

    C. Thousands of banks closed across the country, resulting in them becoming derelict and dusty

    D. A series of dust storms blew across the United States, causing widespread agricultural damage

    E. It is another name for the stock market crash on 'Black Tuesday'

17. **Which of the following was not a cause of the period of fear and paranoia during 1919-20 known as the First Red Scare?**

    A. The Sedition Act

    B. Senator Joseph McCarthy's anti-communist campaigns

    C. Labour strikes

    D. The Haymarket massacre

    E. Bolshevik Russian Revolution

18. **What important Civil Rights Movement incident lasted for over a year from 1955 in Montgomery, Alabama?**

    A. A series of church bombings occurred, killing many in the black community

    B. A march was led from Montgomery to Washington, where Martin Luther King gave his "I have a dream" speech

    C. Refusal of the black community to ride on segregated buses

    D. Four black college students engaged in 'sit-ins' at a number of restaurants where black patrons were not served

    E. Riots were held in a local university over the enrolment of the school's first black student, until federal troops were sent to enforce the law

19. **Which bilateral conferences occurred between the USA and Soviet Union in the 1970s to reach agreements on the control of nuclear armaments?**

    A. The Strategic Arms Limitation Talks

    B. The Committee on Disarmament Conference

    C. The Hague Peace Conference

    D. The Washington Atomic Treaty

    E. The Nuclear Weapons Convention

20. **Which Act of Congress was passed in 2001 to assist in the monitoring and detainment of terrorists, and continues to this day?**

    A. The Stolen Valor Act

    B. The CAN-SPAM Act

    C. The PROTECT Act

    D. The Risk-Based Security Screening Act

    E. The PATRIOT Act

21. The "Great Famine" of 1845-1852 caused hundreds of thousands of people from which nation to immigrate to the USA?

   A. Germany

   B. Spain

   C. China

   D. Ireland

   E. Mexico

22. What was *Pax Romana*?

   A. A period of peace and stability experienced by those within the Roman Empire

   B. A romantic Roman play about Marc Antony's relationship with Cleopatra

   C. A failed Roman military campaign against Scotland

   D. A network of trade routes that connected Rome with Central Asia

   E. A tax enforced by the Roman Empire

23. The wealth of the Dutch Empire was largely built from shipping and trade to the profitable colonies of the Dutch East India Company, one of the earliest multi-national corporations. Which of the following was a colony of the Dutch East India Company?

   A. Batavia, now Jakarta

   B. Goa

   C. Singapore

   D. Hong Kong

   E. Seychelles

24. Which of the following describes a feudal system?

   A. The king did not own the land, but divided it between his barons into numerous independent states

   B. Knights farmed the land for their barons

   C. Peasants vote to elect their leaders

   D. The church belongs to the people

   E. The noble or lord has power

25. Which individual led armies that created an empire stretching from the Danube in Europe to Egypt, and as far east as India in the 4th century BCE?

   A. Hannibal

   B. Cyrus the Great

   C. Alexander the Great

   D. Qin Shi Huang

   E. Julius Caesar

26. In which Greek tragedy by Sophocles (497 – 406 BCE) does the protagonist inadvertently murder his own father and sleep with his mother, fulfilling a prophecy made by the oracle at Delphi?

   A. The Bacchae

   B. Oedipus the King

   C. Medea

   D. The Iliad

   E. Prometheus Bound

27. Which war took place between Athens and Sparta during the 5th century BCE, and was recorded by Thucydides – considered one of the earliest historians?

   A. War of Pyrrhus

   B. Alexander the Great's campaign

   C. Greco-Persian War

   D. Peloponnesian War

   E. Trojan War

28. Which group of Turks ruled an enormous empire from Mesopotamia to Iran during the time of the First and Second Crusades, before being defeated by the Mongols at the Battle of Köse Dağ (1243)?

   A. Uyghurs

   B. Ottomans

   C. Mamluks

   D. Seljuks

   E. Ayyubids

29. **In November 1095 Pope Urban II gave a sermon to the French aristocracy at the Council of Clermont. The following year, what military campaign began?**

    A. The First Crusade

    B. The War of the Spanish Succession

    C. The First Balkan War

    D. The conquest of Gaul

    E. The invasion of Northern Germany

30. **During the Age of Enlightenment, which event resulted in William of Orange invading England, overthrowing the king, and forever changing the structure of the British monarchy by inextricably linking monarchic with parliamentary power?**

    A. The Fronde (1648 - 1653)

    B. The Glorious Revolution (1688)

    C. Pontiac's Rebellion (1763 - 1766)

    D. The Jacobite risings (1688 - 1746)

    E. The Camisard Rebellion (1702 - 1715)

31. **Who wrote *The Wealth of Nations* in 1776?**

    A. John Keynes

    B. Karl Marx

    C. Irving Fisher

    D. John Locke

    E. Adam Smith

32. **Which of the following is an appropriate explanation of humanism, as developed during the Renaissance?**

    A. The belief that man can live an ethical and civil life on Earth by studying moral philosophy, history, rhetoric and poetry from Greek and Roman sources

    B. The belief that people as a whole should not be able to read, write, debate, or question how the people are managed

    C. The belief that humans evolved from primates, diverging about 85 million years ago

    D. The belief that we can learn nothing from Classical, pagan works of art, other than how past cultures were hedonistic

    E. The belief that we can trust certain, educated, elite individuals to properly understand the world and promote how we should live

33. **During the early 16th century Pope Leo X sold indulgences in order to pay for the reconstruction of St. Peter's Basilica in Rome. What are indulgences, in this case?**

   A. Beautifully illuminated copies of the Bible

   B. Holders did not have to engage in fasting during Lent

   C. Pardons for one's own sins or the sins of their family

   D. Licences to produce wine

   E. Temporarily allowed monks and nuns to engage in sexual encounters

34. **Influenced by both the American Revolution and Enlightenment thought, what important document advocating "natural, unalienable and sacred" human rights was signed in France in August 1789?**

   A. Rights of Man, by Thomas Paine

   B. Code of Hammurabi

   C. Summa Theologica

   D. Magna Carta

   E. Declaration of the Rights of Man and of the Citizen

35. **The French National Day is July 14th, when it celebrates what event of the French Revolution that occurred in 1789?**

   A. French occupation of Nice

   B. Storming of the Bastille

   C. Napoleon's Egyptian expedition

   D. The fall of Robespierre after the period known as 'the Terror'

   E. Louis XVI beheaded

36. **At which battle did the British destroy Napoleon Bonaparte's fleet in 1805?**

   A. Trafalgar

   B. Somme

   C. Gallipoli

   D. Culloden

   E. Waterloo

37. **Which of the following was the most immediate result of the February Revolution in Russia in 1917?**

   A. The formation of the USSR

   B. The Grand Duke of Muscovy took power

   C. Peter I (commonly known as 'the Great') responded by modernizing the Russian army

   D. Abdication of Tsar Nicholas II

   E. Execution of the Romanov family

38. **In 1917, Vladimir Lenin started an organisation called the Cheka which was dissolved in 1922. What was the Cheka's role?**

   A. A group in charge of stimulating peaceful diplomatic relations with the Germans

   B. Build a trans-Siberian railroad to Vladivostok

   C. The governmental department in charge of collectivizing farms

   D. Early Soviet secret police

   E. Radio station primarily used to promote propaganda

39. **The Pyramid of Cheops was built by the Pharaoh Khufu during the Old Kingdom of Egypt (3rd millennium BCE) on the Giza Plateau, and is famous around the world as one of the Seven Wonders of the Ancient World. Which of the following monumental structures is also found on the Giza Plateau?**

   A. Luxor Temple

   B. Valley of the Kings

   C. Temple of Hatshepsut

   D. Abu Simbel

   E. Great Sphinx

40. **In what area of the world did the Second Boer War (1899 – 1910) between the United Kingdom and the Orange Free State take place?**

   A. South Africa

   B. Turkey

   C. Argentina

   D. France

   E. Belgium

41. The famous 9th century temple of Borobudur in Java, Indonesia, was a monument for which religion?

    A. Islam

    B. Daoism

    C. Shinto

    D. Buddhism

    E. Christianity

42. Over 40 countries lay claim UNESCO's World Heritage status from having been involved in the material and cultural movements of the land- and maritime-based Silk Roads. Which of the following countries did the 'Silk Road' not pass through?

    A. India

    B. Iran

    C. Morocco

    D. Jordan

    E. China

43. What was the "Mandate of Heaven"?

    A. The name of Horatio Nelson's flagship, on which he was shot and died during the Napoleonic Wars

    B. A plot device used in ancient Greek and Roman plays to suddenly solve or conclude a seemingly unsolvable issue

    C. A document nailed to the door of All Saints' Church in Wittenberg by Martin Luther, which is believed to have started the Protestant Reformation

    D. An ancient Chinese concept of legitimacy used by the emperors to justify their rule

    E. The approval given by the Spanish crown to Christopher Columbus to make his first voyage west

44. Which Chinese admiral embarked with a fleet of over three hundred ships on a series of seven exploratory voyages around Southeast Asia and East Africa the in the early 15th century?

    A. Xuanzang

    B. Hong Xiuquan

    C. Marco Polo

    D. Jiang Zemin

    E. Zheng He

45.   **What did the Treaty of Versailles accomplish?**

A.   Partitioned the Carolingian Empire

B.   Ended the First World War

C.   Ended the Thirty Years War

D.   Created the Vatican City as an independent state

E.   Ended the Russo-Japanese War

46.   **The Russo-Japanese War (1904 – 1905) formally ended with the Treaty of Portsmouth. Which of the following is an accurate result of this war?**

A.   Russia's victory was met with sympathy and support by countries throughout the rest of East and South-East Asia, as well as confirming Western imperial superiority over non-Western powers.

B.   Japan was awarded the northern part of Sakhalin Island, though had to concede its presence in Port Arthur, Manchuria and Korea to Russia

C.   The Tsar agreed to pay indemnities to Japan, in return for keeping the important strategic location of Port Arthur and the endpoint of the Trans-Siberian Railway

D.   The Meiji Emperor's defeat forced Japan to remove their presence from Manchuria and Korea, causing them to abandon their efforts to establish imperial hegemony in East Asia and undergo a further decade of isolationism

E.   The southern half of Sakhalin Island, Southern Manchuria and Korea were ceded to the Japanese, forcing Russia to withdraw as the country faced internal revolution

47. **Francisco Pizarro was a Spanish conquistador that conquered which South American empire in the 16th century?**

    A. Incan

    B. Assyrian

    C. Teotihuacan

    D. Mayan

    E. Aztec

48. **Which of the following is a result of the 1949 Chinese Communist Revolution?**

    A. Political power in China became unified under a stable republic led by Yuan Shikai

    B. Chiang Kai-shek proclaimed Taipei, Taiwan, as the capital of the communist People's Republic of China

    C. It sparked the "Great Leap Forward" the following year, which aimed to transform China into a socialist society

    D. Liu Shaoqi was elected as the first Premier of the People's Republic of China, and spent the following decade establishing diplomatic links with the USA.

    E. Political power in China became divided between two parties: the People's Republic of China led by Mao Zedong and the Kuomintang led by Chiang Kai-shek

49. **The Commonwealth Games is an international sporting event that is celebrated every four years by athletes from the Commonwealth of Nations. The Commonwealth of Nations is composed of which of the following?**

    A. All members of the League of Nations

    B. Countries that possess one or more UNESCO World Heritage Sites

    C. Former and current territories of the British Empire

    D. Member-countries of the Olympic Council of Asia

    E. All countries in the Arab League

50. When referring to Canada as a realm in the Commonwealth of Nations, which of the following is an ongoing diplomatic link between Canada and the United Kingdom?

A. The UK is aiding Canada's attempts in becoming a member of the G20 by 2016

B. Both countries were founding members of the League of Nations

C. Both countries are members of the Organization of American States

D. Over the last decade the UK has become Canada's largest source of immigration

E. Both countries share the same monarch as head of state, Queen Elizabeth II

51. Debates between Germany and Greece over how to overcome the Greek debt crisis have intensified since 2009, and have worsened since Greece failed to make their International Monetary fund (IMF) repayment in June 2015. One contentious solution pursued by the recent Greek Prime Minister Alexis Tsipras is a €278.7bn payment from Germany, for which of the following reasons?

A. To boost Greece's tourism sector, which has been overtaken by Germany's

B. German taxpayers are amongst the worst in Europe for outstanding tax debts, and are thus hypocrites

C. Germany has a lower population than Greece, but is much richer and can thus afford to spare the funding

D. It will let Germany off from funding other potentially indebted governments in the future

E. Germany owes war reparations as compensation for Nazi activities in Greece during World War II

52. **When you plead the Fifth Amendment, what are you doing?**

    A. Defending your right to vote as an individual aged over 18

    B. Defending your right not to be enslaved

    C. Defending your right to bear arms

    D. Refuse to answer a question to prevent self-incrimination

    E. Refusing to allow an unreasonable search or seizure of property

53. **Why is the constitution known as a "living document"?**

    A. It cannot be amended any more

    B. It was written on vellum (animal hide), rather than paper

    C. It can dynamically change and be edited depending on the current social context

    D. It continues to reflect the values of its initial 39 signatories

    E. It applies to all citizens of the United States

54. **What does "naturalization" mean?**

    A. For a non-citizen to become a recognized citizen of a state

    B. The conquering and subsequent transformation of a nation-state by one of a different political structure, e.g. communism to democracy

    C. The process by which an urban zone becomes redefined as a rural zone

    D. To advocate and practice social nudity

    E. An educational campaign that promotes heterosexuality

55. **What does 'gerrymandering' refer to?**

    A. Illegally tapping communication networks, such as mobile telephones or internet connections, with the intention of blackmailing the victim

    B. It is another word for door-to-door canvassing during a political campaign

    C. Manipulating electoral district boundaries in order to achieve an advantageous result for one party

    D. The annual burning of an effigy in the form on a particularly despised politician, as a form of protest

    E. Bribing or otherwise incentivising a group of people to vote for a certain official

56. Which of the following is an example of a welfare state?

A. Egypt

B. Brazil

C. The United Kingdom

D. Russia

E. India

57. What are "checks and balances", as established by the constitution?

A. Ensuring no single branch of government has an unfair advantage or becomes too independent or powerful, by giving other branches the ability to limit the other's actions.

B. Maintains that all people should be treated equally, regardless of race, colour, gender, physical or mental ability, or religion

C. Gives members of the government freedom to independently implement their policies by providing funding, for which they must apply with a proposal

D. Guarantees a regular supply of money to the country, by making it illegal to destroy cash or print your own currency

E. Gives US citizens the right to manage their own banking affairs through web-banking platforms, though not all banks provide this

58. Which of the following most accurately describes a socialist government?

A. A government ruled by those who seek to enforce the will of God

B. Active and controlling role in the economy with many government institutions

C. Government is almost absent, with the individual freedom of the people emphasised, allowing them to make their own economic decisions

D. A prime minister is head of state, in which they can influence the economy for only as long as they remain elected

E. Small groups of leaders elected for their intelligence and wealth, who play a minimal role in society

59. What is "Common Law", when referring to the United States and England?

A. Regulations that restrict a government's ability to make drastic changes to the political system

B. Laws made by collective legislature, resulting in the creation of a formal written statute

C. The resolution of disputes between these two countries at a neutral international court

D. System of courts that applies the law to the "common" people

E. Judicial laws that derive their legitimacy from norms and customs developed gradually over time

60. Which of the following is an accurate description of "Manifest Destiny", as promoted in the USA?

A. The belief that sovereignty is granted by the people, in exchange for protection afforded to them by the government

B. The right of the American president to be re-elected, so as to give them an opportunity to complete their policies

C. The belief that Americans should not be bound by British law

D. The belief that heaven had granted US presidents the right to rule based on their moral authority

E. The right of the American government to stretch their power over the entire continent, from coast to coast

61. What did the 1789 Judiciary Act achieve?

A. Provided federal land grants to adults

B. Established the federal court system

C. Introduced the "separate but equal" doctrine

D. Allowed citizenship in the United States by birth or naturalization

E. Enabled the direct election of senators

62. **What was the major result of the 1965 Voting Rights Act?**

    A. Prevented racial discrimination in voting

    B. Gave Native Americans the right to vote

    C. Gave overseas citizens the right to vote

    D. Gave women the right to vote

    E. Abolished property requirements to vote for all men

63. **Which of the following describes "suffrage"?**

    A. The right to citizenship

    B. The right to education

    C. The right to vote

    D. The right to be free from suffering

    E. The right to free speech

64. **Medieval maps of the world are known by what name? They often serve as minor encyclopaedias, with navigational accuracy sacrificed for illustrative classical imagery.**

    A. Archaeomaps

    B. Kunyu Quantu

    C. Dymaxion maps

    D. Mappa Mundi

    E. Choropleth maps

65. **'Mercator' is an example of what type of map projection? It provides greater accuracy around the equator, decreasing in accuracy the further away from this central line.**

    A. Polyhedral

    B. Cylindrical

    C. Azimuthal

    D. Conic

    E. None of the above

66. **The concentric zone model, developed by Ernest Burgess in 1925, is most commonly used to examine what?**

    A. Urbanization

    B. Precipitation

    C. Place names

    D. Traffic flow

    E. Death rates

67. **When referring to the use of Geographic Information Systems (GIS), which of the following is not true about rasters?**

    A. Naturally good at handling image data

    B. Ideal for analysis of landscape

    C. Space is divided into cells of the same size (tessellation)

    D. Data is stored in a matrix

    E. Good for studying clearly bounded entities

68. **There have been several proposals throughout history for creating a bridge over which body of water separating Russia from Alaska?**

    A. Dardanelles

    B. Bering Strait

    C. Great Belt

    D. Naruto Strait

    E. Alas Strait

69. **The contiguous United States are composed of _____.**

    A. Alaska, Hawaii, and any overseas territories

    B. 50 U.S. states, the District of Columbia, and any overseas territories

    C. 48 U.S. states and the District of Columbia

    D. 50 U.S. states and the District of Columbia

    E. 52 U.S. states and the District of Columbia

70. **Which of these was a result of divergent plate tectonics?**

    A. San Andreas Fault

    B. Andes mountain range

    C. The island of Iceland

    D. Japan

    E. The Himalaya mountain range

71. Swash, backwash, prevailing wind, and transportation of sand are all features of which coastal phenomenon?

   A. Melting ice caps

   B. Blowholes

   C. Wave cut platforms

   D. Wave refraction

   E. Longshore drift

72. Afghanistan can be described as going through the second stage of the Demographic Transition Model, otherwise known as the early expanding stage. Which of these are true for this stage?

   A. High birth rate, falling death rate, rising population

   B. Low birth rate, high death rate, falling population

   C. Low birth rate, low death rate, rising population

   D. High birth rate, low death rate, falling population

   E. High birth rate, high death rate, low and stagnant population

73. What name is Southern Italy otherwise known by? The region is widely studied as part of a North-South economic divide in the country, due in part to widespread corruption and violence by the mafia.

   A. Piedmont

   B. Isole

   C. Centro

   D. Mezzogiorno

   E. Settentrione

74. A study is made that estimates changes to network traffic following the widespread adoption of fibre-optic cables. This was in response to local demand for faster internet. What type of spatial analysis is the study likely to use when examining issues of accessibility and connectivity?

   A. Spatial interpolation

   B. Complete spatial randomness

   C. Spatial epidemiology

   D. Spatial interaction

   E. Spatial regression

75. **In which country is the caste system prevalent?**

    A. Russia

    B. Mexico

    C. Egypt

    D. China

    E. India

76. **Which terrestrial biome exhibits these characteristics: permanently frozen soil, low precipitation, and low temperature? Example flora includes shrubs, lichens and mosses. Example fauna includes hares, wolves, and an absence of reptiles.**

    A. Mangrove

    B. Temperate coniferous forests

    C. Tundra

    D. Semiarid savanna

    E. Xeric shrubland

77. **The current capital city of Turkey has been known by many names since its founding in the 7ᵗʰ century BCE. Which of the following has not been a name of the city?**

    A. Byzantium

    B. Constantinople

    C. Istanbul

    D. Stamboul

    E. Alexandria

78. **Which of the following would not normally cause a supply shock?**

    A. Discovery that a certain brand of aspirin causes cancer

    B. Foot and mouth disease hitting a herd of cattle

    C. Adoption of robots providing increased productivity in a car factory

    D. Hurricane Katrina sweeping over an industrial estate

    E. Discovery of a cheaper substitute for gasoline

79. **What does PED stand for, in the economic sense of a commodity's ability to adapt its supply or cost based on changing circumstances?**

    A. Penny Extension Drive

    B. Price Elasticity of Demand

    C. Performance Enhancing Demand

    D. Pressured Economics Directive

    E. Personal Emergency Demand

80. **A market is in equilibrium when:**

   A. Quantity of goods supplied is in excess of the quantity demanded

   B. Quantity of goods supplied is below the quantity demanded

   C. Buyers spend all of their money

   D. Excess demand is zero

   E. Price ceilings stop restricting free market prices

81. **Which of the following is an argument that supports the idea that university students should have to pay for their own fees, rather than the taxpayer?**

   A. The top universities are not under too much pressure, and could comfortably accept on many new students

   B. It encourages the proliferation of less conventional university courses, such as 'Surf Science and Technology'

   C. It will scare off international students, meaning that universities can accept more local students

   D. The state has more than enough money to spare, and should offer subsidies for education

   E. They are deriving private benefit from the experience, and will be the sole ones to gain from the education

82. **Which of the following is not a member of the OPEC (Organization of the Petroleum Exporting Countries)?**

   A. Iran

   B. Iraq

   C. Afghanistan

   D. Saudi Arabia

   E. Venezuela

83. **The German government suddenly decides to impose a minimum price for Sauerkraut that is below the existing market price. The existing market price was originally higher than the equilibrium price, but what effect will this change have?**

   A. Increases supply, as manufacturers are making more of a profit

   B. Decreases supply, as manufacturers are operating on a loss

   C. Causes demand to decrease

   D. Customers now have to pay higher prices for the goods

   E. It has no effect

84. **The USA acquires most of its oil from _____**

   A. The USA

   B. Mexico

   C. The United Arab Emirates

   D. Israel

   E. Iraq

85. **What is a laissez-faire economic system?**

   A. One in which government has a total, authoritarian control over its people

   B. One in which government provides a lot of welfare

   C. One in which members of government are given special privileges and subsidies

   D. One in which government enforces widespread regulations and tariffs

   E. One in which government stays out of economic affairs

86. **When we raise the price of a product, the _____ states that this will lower the quantity required of the product.**

   A. Law of reflux

   B. Okun's law

   C. Law of demand

   D. Law of profit

   E. Law of quantity

87. **Which of the following would not cause changes to a demand curve?**

   A. Changes in taste

   B. Changes in the price of the good itself

   C. Changes in consumer incomes

   D. Changes in the price of related goods

   E. Changes in preference

88. A person is late for work, and decides to drive in order to make up time. However, it appears that everybody else has thought of the same thing, and the driver finds that the roads are extremely congested. Which of the following would not be an appropriate description of this shared abuse of public roads – resulting in it being harmful for the group as a whole?

A. Overexploitation

B. Zelinsky Model of Migration Transition

C. Chain reaction

D. Social trap

E. Tragedy of the Commons

89. China's per capita water resources are only 28% of the global average, which is one of the lowest levels in the world. The scarcity of water in China today, especially drinking water, has had a devastating effect upon which of the following?

A. China's annual GDP

B. growth in China's cities

C. infant mortality in rural villages

D. accelerated shrinking of lakes and drying of rivers

E. all of the above

90. Which psychological model describes the development of long-term interpersonal relationships, such as that between a mother and child, and in particular how humans respond when that relationship is threatened?

A. Maslow's hierarchy of needs

B. Kohlberg's stages of moral development

C. Attachment theory

D. Triarchic theory of intelligence

E. Theory of multiple intelligences

91. **An individual constantly exaggerates their own self-importance, clearly indicates that they want to be desired by everyone, and at the same time rarely shows empathy for others. These could indicate a _____**

A. Schizotypal personality disorder

B. Avoidant personality disorder

C. Borderline personality disorder

D. Paranoid personality disorder

E. Narcissistic personality disorder

92. **Which of the following does the brain produce in its normal state when an individual is awake during the day?**

A. Beta waves

B. Delta waves

C. Gamma waves

D. Zeta waves

E. Theta waves

93. **_____ is best known for focusing on the dynamics between the id, ego and superego with their psychoanalytical approach?**

A. Jean Piaget

B. Sigmund Freud

C. Carl Rogers

D. Ivan Pavlov

E. Kurt Lewin

94. **Which of the following is an example of impulsive-aggressive behaviour?**

A. Two siblings get into an argument over whose turn it is to play on the video game console, and they resolve the situation by talking it out and reaching a compromise

B. A school group bully a member of the class by gossiping behind their back, and always pretends to be nice whenever the individual is in their presence

C. A member of Jane's family always rolls their eyes whenever she says something silly

D. An individual is very insulted by a statement they overhear, but decide to ignore it and move on

E. A car driver has to brake suddenly when a cyclist cuts in front. The driver of the car sounds their horn, shouts angrily, and speeds up so as to intimidate the cyclist.

95. Who created a theory of cognitive development that explores the influence childhood has on the development of a person's intelligence?

A. Ivan Pavlov

B. Albert Bandura

C. Jean Piaget

D. Sigmund Freud

E. F. Skinner

96. What is a control group?

A. A group that creates the research plan, and ensures that it stays on track

B. A group of shareholders that funds research

C. A group that receives no treatment during an experiment

D. A group that is studied, but the results of which are ignored in the final synthesis

E. A group that is complete control over what takes place during an experiment

97. A schoolchild learns that when they receive good grades in class they will be rewarded by their parents with a trip to the cinema, but if they receive poor grades the trip to the cinema is withdrawn. This is an example of:

A. Innateness theory

B. Phylogeny

C. Classical conditioning

D. Operant conditioning

E. Ethology

98. An individual is convinced that a slight headache they are experiencing means that they possess a brain tumour. They are not faking the symptoms, but what somatoform disorder may they be experiencing?

A. Hypochondria

B. Kleptomania

C. Dyspareunia

D. Bulimia nervosa

E. Erotomania

99. **We are able to visualize the world in three dimensions because of which ability?**

    A. Nociception

    B. Peripheral vision

    C. Chronoception

    D. Vestibular sense

    E. Depth perception

100. **Which theory maintains that people's actions are motivated by their biological impulses?**

    A. Drive reduction theory

    B. Disposition deterioration theory

    C. Instinct decline theory

    D. Impulse decrease theory

    E. Motivation collapse theory

101. **What is meant by describing someone as being conscientious?**

    A. They have a tendency to promote a certain point of view above all others

    B. They have a tendency to be self-disciplined and organized

    C. They have a tendency to exaggerate their own merits or importance

    D. They have a tendency to be extremely self-aware, through regular meditation

    E. They have a tendency to be lazy and unreliable

102. Which of the following is an example of cultural lag?

A. The technological advancement of smartphones is being readily accepted by global society, resulting in features such as touchscreens, cameras, and access to social networking being made available to a growing number of the world's population.

B. Although their status has changed in recent decades, the rights of women in Saudi Arabia are denounced by some other nations as being extremely limited, although they are considered normal and acceptable by the conservative majority within that nation.

C. A European student is attending an exchange program at a school in Beijing, and feels extremely confused, nervous and disoriented for the first few weeks of living there. This is because they react to elements of Chinese culture differently, such as unusual food, the unfamiliar language and public spitting.

D. Many members of 19th century European imperial powers, such as the British Empire and Dutch Empire, which occupied lands in Asia, Africa and the Americas, believed that the indigenous cultures were largely primitive and would benefit from their colonial presence.

E. The fertilisation of a mother's egg occurs in a laboratory environment, using the donated sperm of an unknown male. This is not fully accepted by most of society, and protests occur due to long-established ideas of parenthood, as well as ongoing debates over potential social, psychological, and legal harm that this procedure might cause.

103. Which of the following would not make an appropriate study using a conflict-theory perspective?

A. How youth crime's relation to mainstream values being imposed on them

B. How a nation went through stages of feudalism, capitalism and socialism throughout their history

C. How social cohesion is enforced by institutions in a society

D. The factors leading to a divide between those who are most wealthy in society and those who primarily engage in labour

E. How the main economic "classes" of the nation/world create society by clashing

104. **In 1991, Clark McPhail's study of collective behaviour *The Myth of the Madding Crowd* identified a number of types of convergent and collective behaviour – known as his 'assembling perspective'. Which of the following is an example of collective locomotion?**

    A. The audience at a conference all facing the speaker

    B. Everybody screams when a roller coaster begins to plunge

    C. A marching band carrying their array of instruments

    D. A congregation speaking *The Lord's Prayer* in church

    E. Jumping for joy when your favourite sports team scores a point

105. **Which of the following is a latent function of education?**

    A. Taught the duties of a patriotism and citizenship

    B. Identify what your position in society may be after school, based on your talents

    C. Realize the importance of punctuality and self-discipline

    D. Started dating your classmate, who became your life-long partner

    E. Taught the value of discipline by your teacher

106. **Sociologists have noticed that in many modern nations gerontocracy has been reduced, changing the social standing of certain groups of people in terms of wealth, prestige, and job opportunities. In a gerontocratic society, who would have the most power and influence?**

    A. Children of the previous rulers

    B. The oldest members of society

    C. Younger males

    D. Women who have had at least one child

    E. Nobody has more power – it is shared amongst all members of the adult population

107. **Mothers Against Drunk Driving (MADD) is a national group attempting to change one specific thing about the social structure: to stop drunk driving. What type of social movement is this?**

    A. Resistance movement

    B. Religious movement

    C. Revolutionary movement

    D. Alternative movement

    E. Reform movement

108. This sociologist's book, *The Elementary Forms of the Religious Life* (1912), studied the role of religion in social life by looking at totemism in Aboriginal Australian communities. Who are they?

A. Émile Durkheim

B. Michel Foucault

C. Erving Goffman

D. Daniel Bell

E. Charles Wright Mills

109. What social movement started in the 1960s, continued for two decades, and resulted in the formation of the National Organization for Women?

A. Second Wave Feminism

B. Anti-consumerism

C. Arab Spring

D. Women's Suffrage Movement

E. Occupy Wall Street

110. Which of the following studies would a social epidemiologist be least likely to study?

A. Study how people from different countries around the world react to flu germs

B. Examining health disparities based on gender within a school

C. Observe how changes in religious beliefs impact the breakdown of the traditional authority of the church

D. Critically evaluate a popular paper that claims to provide a homeopathic cure for diabetes, by investigating demographics that believe it

E. How the communal nature of Thanksgiving dinners impact the risk of obesity in a group

111. A student does not get the required test scores to move on to the next grade; however their teacher decides to move them up anyway in order for them in their intended social group. This is an example of _____.

A. Dropping out

B. Merit promotion

C. Summer school

D. Grade retention

E. Social promotion

112. In August 1942 the Bracero Program was initiated, resulting in the widespread immigration of which "group"?

A. Irish

B. Chinese

C. Polish

D. Mexicans

E. Brazilians

113. Which of the following is not the dominant religion in the country?

A. India – Hinduism

B. Israel – Judaism

C. Argentina – Catholicism

D. Iran – Buddhism

E. Saudi Arabia – Islam

114. What is the reasoning behind the 'law of superposition', which is the basis of much archaeological and geological investigation?

A. Anything discovered automatically belongs to the country in which the investigation took place

B. The age of material remains is indicated by their stratigraphic position, with the bottom layers being the oldest and upper layers being the youngest.

C. It is a statement indicating the research project's strategy and methods, allowing the researchers to keep focused on specific goals

D. 'Experts', usually academically trained, are no longer the only ones that may engage in such investigation – increasingly the public are involved

E. Surveying provides limited information, so it is only through excavation that they can fully understand a site

115. Bronislaw Malinowski was an anthropologist best known for promoting which theoretical approach to social anthropology that emphasises how cultures exists to meet the cultural and psychological needs of individuals?

A. Functionalism

B. Postmodernism

C. Marxism

D. Darwinism

E. Cartesian dualism

116. A survey of an historic landscape is made by a research team. The team is split into smaller groups, who cover a very large area in a short period of time. They use representative sampling strategies, and ensure that nothing on the landscape is touched or disturbed – only recorded. This is an example of:

A. An intensive, non-intrusive survey

B. An extensive, intrusive survey

C. An extensive, non-intrusive survey

D. An intensive, intrusive survey

E. None of the above

117. What bias exists in the ways "Asia" has been perceived as distinct from "the West"? Edward Said used this term in his seminal book of the same name to describe how our assumptions of "the East" are actually enduring creations by European scholars, writers and observers during periods of colonial domination – changing how scholars think about power, culture, history and identity formation.

A. Axiology

B. Barbarianism

C. Indology

D. Orientalism

E. Occidentalism

118. _____ is a culture's ideas of the origins of the universe, and includes beliefs on how the world and living things were created, our 'place' in the universe, and how the universe 'works'. In some cultures the influences of spiritual, non-corporeal forces play a large role.

A. Syncretism

B. Osmosis

C. Levelling mechanism

D. Astrology

E. Cosmology

119. **Which of the following approaches believes that one has to study all aspects of a culture in order to fully understand it?**

     A. Phenomenological approach

     B. Cultural Materialistic approach

     C. Cultural relativistic approach

     D. Functionalist approach

     E. Holistic approach

120. **Which of the following would anthropologists be least likely to study?**

     A. the anatomical features of dinosaurs during the Jurassic Period

     B. changes in the human body and behaviour throughout time

     C. major global transformations throughout history, such as the adoption and spread of agriculture, urbanisation, and industrialisation

     D. a country's economic and political system and opportunities provided to various social groups

     E. the relationship of a religion's material culture with their theological ideologies

ANSWER KEY

Question Number	Correct Answer	Your Answer	Question Number	Correct Answer	Your Answer	Question Number	Correct Answer	Your Answer
1	E		41	D		81	E	
2	C		42	C		82	C	
3	A		43	D		83	B	
4	E		44	E		84	A	
5	B		45	B		85	E	
6	D		46	E		86	C	
7	E		47	A		87	B	
8	B		48	E		88	B	
9	A		49	C		89	E	
10	C		50	E		90	C	
11	C		51	E		91	E	
12	D		52	D		92	A	
13	B		53	C		93	B	
14	A		54	A		94	E	
15	E		55	C		95	C	
16	D		56	C		96	C	
17	B		57	A		97	D	
18	C		58	B		98	A	
19	A		59	E		99	E	
20	E		60	E		100	A	
21	D		61	B		101	B	
22	A		62	A		102	E	
23	A		63	C		103	C	
24	E		64	D		104	E	
25	C		65	B		105	D	
26	B		66	A		106	B	
27	D		67	E		107	E	
28	D		68	B		108	A	
29	A		69	C		109	A	
30	B		70	C		110	C	
31	E		71	E		111	E	
32	A		72	A		112	D	
33	C		73	D		113	D	
34	E		74	D		114	B	
35	B		75	E		115	A	
36	A		76	C		116	C	
37	D		77	E		117	D	
38	D		78	A		118	E	
39	E		79	B		119	E	
40	A		80	D		120	A	

RATIONALES

1. The _____ Incident occurred in August 1964, when two US destroyers were allegedly torpedoed by North Vietnamese, which led to American assistance in South Vietnam – although many claimed, and still maintain, that this was a "false flag" operation.

    A. Ho Chi Minh

    B. Straits of Malacca

    C. Mekong River

    D. Tet Offensive

    E. Gulf of Tonkin

The answer is E.
The Gulf of Tonkin is a bay located between southern China, Hainan Island and northern Vietnam.

2. What did opponents in America call the purchase of Alaska from the Russians in 1867, named after the contemporary Republican Party Secretary of State that orchestrated the move?

    A. Putyatin's Madness

    B. Johnson's Fault

    C. Seward's Folly

    D. Sitka's Scandal

    E. Barker's Blunder

The answer is C.
Many in the USA felt that William Seward was wasting American money on a fruitless venture.

3. **Which nation did the United States fight against in the War of 1812?**

   A. The United Kingdom

   B. Cuba

   C. Japan

   D. Russia

   E. France

The answer is A.

Although the war did not have any effect on either nation's boundaries, it terminated British attempts to create a 'buffer zone' in the USA, and gave future presidents such as Andrew Jackson the military experience they needed to lead America.

4. **Which of the following foreign policies accurately represents the 1947 Truman Doctrine?**

   A. Providing aid to any country that wanted to rollback its political system

   B. Providing aid to the Midwest to improve their healthcare

   C. Providing aid to Southeast Asian nations so they could compete with India

   D. Providing aid to European countries because they were poor

   E. Providing aid to democratic countries to contain the spread of communism

The answer is E.

The Truman Doctrine was focused specifically on the spread of the Soviet sphere of influence, so B and C are false. The key criteria was to support 'free people resisting subjugation' – not necessarily poor nations, so D is false. It was completely against the idea of rollback, whereby a nation's political structure is forcibly changed by another country's regime, so A is false.

5. **In May 1790, Rhode Island became the final state to ratify which of the following documents?**

    A. Homestead Act

    B. Constitution of the United States

    C. Civil Rights Act

    D. Emancipation Proclamation

    E. Declaration of Independence

The answer is B.
Ratification started in 1788, though the first constitution was actually the Articles of Confederation and Perpetual Union (1777). The Homestead Acts and Emancipation Proclamation were ratified in the 19th century, the Civil Rights Act in 1962, and the Declaration of Independence in July 1776.

6. **As a result of United States intervention in the Cuban War of Independence (1895-1898), which of the following countries did the United States declare war on in 1898?**

    A. Canada

    B. Russia

    C. France

    D. Spain

    E. The United Kingdom

The answer is D.
The United States were drawn into the Cuban War of Independence following the sinking of the Maine in 1898, by blaming Spanish officials in Cuba for the incident. In April 1898 Congress decided to send military aid for Cuban independence, and demanded that the Spanish withdraw from the island.

7. **What event are the Sons of Liberty best known for undertaking?**

    A. The assassination of Archduke Franz Ferdinand of Austria, 1914

    B. The Massacre of Wounded Knee, 1890

    C. The Pueblo Revolt, 1680

    D. The River Run Riot, 2002

    E. The Boston Tea Party, 1773

The answer is E.
The Sons of Liberty were a secret society that fought against "taxation without representation".
A is wrong, as this was carried out by the Black Hand secret society. B was carried out by James
Forsyth's 7th Cavalry Regiment. C involved a revolt of the Pueblo people against Spain. D
involved the Hells Angels biker gang.

8. **What was the major result of the American victory against Japan in the Battle of
    Leyte Gulf, Philippines, in 1944?**

    A. The Japanese retaliated by striking at the American fleet stationed at Pearl Harbour

    B. The Japanese fleet was effectively destroyed, causing them to abandon their occupation
        of Southeast Asia and crippling their Pacific naval force

    C. The Japanese army decided that Indonesia and Borneo were easier targets, and invaded
        them the following year in their 'Dutch East Indies campaign'

    D. The Philippines were then divided between America and Japan, allowing each country
        to exploit resources found in the archipelago

    E. The Japanese fleet escaped to their naval bases to refuel before returning in even
        greater numbers in 1946

The answer is B.
Considered the largest naval battle in history, the American fleet terminated Japanese efforts to
occupy Southeast Asia, and was so effective that the Japanese fleet didn't recover before the
Second World War was over.

9. **What does "virtual representation" mean, in the context of the American War of Independence?**

    A. Members of British Parliament claimed to have to the right to speak for and manage the affairs of all British subjects around the world

    B. The claiming of federal land grants by ex-slaves aged 21 years or over

    C. Native American tribes campaigned for their own representatives in the United States government

    D. The United States leadership provided grants of land for third-level educational institutes to train the next generation of politicians

    E. Citizens of the United States wanted the right to vote over the internet and by post

The answer is A.
Members of the British Parliament maintained that they had the right to make political decisions for both their own constituencies and those residing in overseas territories. The American War of Independence was largely caused by resentment felt amongst the population in America towards these policies.

10. **Which U.S. president ordered the invasion of the Bay of Pigs, and in which year?**

    A. Lyndon B. Johnson, 1964

    B. Harry S. Truman, 1962

    C. John F. Kennedy, 1961

    D. Dwight D. Eisenhower, 1960

    E. Richard M. Nixon, 1963

The answer is C.
The Bay of Pigs invasion occurred on 17th April 1961, under the approval of John F. Kennedy. Although Eisenhower was involved in the operation's preparation, the invasion itself took place after Kennedy was elected.

11. **Which event eventually led to the resignation of President Richard Nixon?**

    A. The Florida State Voting Recount

    B. The Chappaquiddick Incident

    C. The Watergate Scandal

    D. The Lewinsky Affair

    E. Abu Ghraib prison abuse

The answer is C.
This act of espionage against the Democratic National Committee was initially not believed to have been connected with President Nixon, but when the cover-up failed it forced the president to resign, rather than face impeachment.

12. **Which Native American tribe separated from the Shoshone after the Pueblo Revolt (1680), and were famous for their prowess on horseback? They occupied the southwest Great Plains, and today mainly reside in Oklahoma, Texas and New Mexico.**

    A. Apache

    B. Wampanoag

    C. Ojibwe

    D. Comanche

    E. Sioux

The answer is D.
Although they are believed to have been present in the southern United States during the 17th century, the Apache were not subjects of the Shoshone, but instead were already a distinct and independent group at the time of the revolt. The Wampanoag tribe occupied south-eastern Massachusetts and Rhode Island, and the Ojibwe were mostly found in the northern United States and Canada. The Sioux were mostly present in the Dakotas and Minnesota. After the Pueblo Revolt the Comanche separated from the Shoshone and settled in Wyoming.

13. **Following the Indian Removal Act (1830), a number of Native American nations were forcibly relocated from their ancestral homelands in the American Southeast to "Indian Territory" west of the Mississippi. By what name is this event known as?**

    A. The Quetta Annexation

    B. The Trail of Tears

    C. The Expulsion of the Moriscos

    D. The Highland Clearances

    E. The Santiago de Compostela

The answer is B.
It was given this name based on an account of the forced relocation of the Choctaw people.

14. **What did the Thirteenth Amendment to the Constitution, passed in December 1865, accomplish?**

    A. Abolition of slavery, except as punishment for a crime

    B. Protected the right to keep and bear arms

    C. The right to be secure against unreasonable searches and seizures

    D. Began electing US Senators by popular vote

    E. Provided the right to trial by jury

The answer is A.
One year after Lincoln's *Emancipation Proclamation*, which advocated the universal freedom of slaves in all but the Union's Border States, the amendment was passed by Congress. It was immediately ratified by eighteen states in 1865, with most of the other existing states adopting it over the following five years.

15. **Which of the following occurred between 1800 and 1900?**

    A. George Washington died

    B. New Mexico became the 47th US state

    C. Native Americans given the right to vote

    D. The Wall Street Crash

    E. The *Cross of Gold* speech was delivered by William Jennings Bryan

The answer is E.
Bryan's speech was a bitter invective against the gold standard, and promoted the adoption of a silver coinage to inflate the economy, leading to his presidential election, though he was never elected. A occurred in 1799, B occurred in 1912, C occurred in 1965 with the Voting Rights Act, and D occurred in 1929.

16. **What was the "Dust Bowl", which had a phenomenal influence on the severity of the Great Depression?**

    A. An act passed which raised import duties for alcohol, causing widespread protests by those in need of drink

    B. A giant curved dam was built at Grand Rapids, Michigan, which caused major rivers to dry up and the water table to sink

    C. Thousands of banks closed across the country, resulting in them becoming derelict and dusty

    D. A series of dust storms blew across the United States, causing widespread agricultural damage

    E. It is another name for the stock market crash on 'Black Tuesday'

The answer is D.
Enormous clouds of dust were formed by a combination of strong winds and a severe drought, ruining millions of acres of agricultural land, and causing thousands of farming families to lose their livelihood.

17. **Which of the following was not a cause of the period of fear and paranoia during 1919-20 known as the First Red Scare?**

    A. The Sedition Act

    B. Senator Joseph McCarthy's anti-communist campaigns

    C. Labour strikes

    D. The Haymarket massacre

    E. Bolshevik Russian Revolution

The answer is B.
"McCarthyism" took place during the second Red Scare.

18. **What important Civil Rights Movement incident lasted for over a year from 1955 in Montgomery, Alabama?**

    A. A series of church bombings occurred, killing many in the black community

    B. A march was led from Montgomery to Washington, where Martin Luther King gave his "I have a dream" speech

    C. Refusal of the black community to ride on segregated buses

    D. Four black college students engaged in 'sit-ins' at a number of restaurants where black patrons were not served

    E. Riots were held in a local university over the enrolment of the school's first black student, until federal troops were sent to enforce the law

The answer is C.
Following the arrest of Rosa Parks in December 1955, the Montgomery Bus Boycott crippled the city's bus network by providing cheap taxis and carpools to the black community. It ended with the Browder v. Gayle court ruling in 1956, which stated that the state's bus segregation laws were unconstitutional.

19. **Which bilateral conferences occurred between the USA and Soviet Union in the 1970s to reach agreements on the control of nuclear armaments?**

    A. The Strategic Arms Limitation Talks

    B. The Committee on Disarmament Conference

    C. The Hague Peace Conference

    D. The Washington Atomic Treaty

    E. The Nuclear Weapons Convention

The answer is A.

These conferences occurred twice: the first resulted in the successful Anti-Ballistic Missile Treaty regarding ICBM missiles; the second round's negotiations were on the further reduction of nuclear missiles.

20. **Which Act of Congress was passed in 2001 to assist in the monitoring and detainment of terrorists, and continues to this day?**

    A. The Stolen Valor Act

    B. The CAN-SPAM Act

    C. The PROTECT Act

    D. The Risk-Based Security Screening Act

    E. The PATRIOT Act

The answer is E.

The PATRIOT Act serves to secure the country against terrorism, by facilitating a range of surveillance procedures, anti-money laundering measures, enhanced border security and more.

21. **The "Great Famine" of 1845-1852 caused hundreds of thousands of people from which nation to immigrate to the USA?**

    A. Germany

    B. Spain

    C. China

    D. Ireland

    E. Mexico

The answer is D.
The "Great Famine" of 1845-1852 occurred in Ireland, and was caused by the potato blight which destroyed the main source of food of around 40% of the population. This resulted in the deaths of hundreds of thousands, and the emigration of almost one million Irish around the world.

22. **What was *Pax Romana*?**

    A. A period of peace and stability experienced by those within the Roman Empire

    B. A romantic Roman play about Marc Antony's relationship with Cleopatra

    C. A failed Roman military campaign against Scotland

    D. A network of trade routes that connected Rome with Central Asia

    E. A tax enforced by the Roman Empire

The answer is A.
Those within imperial Rome experienced a prolonged period of peace brought on by effective control of the frontier, apart from a few minor rebellions. This facilitated a widespread assimilation of cultures into the Empire.

23. **The wealth of the Dutch Empire was largely built from shipping and trade to the profitable colonies of the Dutch East India Company, one of the earliest multi-national corporations. Which of the following was a colony of the Dutch East India Company?**

   A. Batavia, now Jakarta

   B. Goa

   C. Singapore

   D. Hong Kong

   E. Seychelles

The answer is A.
Batavia was the capital city of the Dutch East Indies. Goa was a colony of the Portuguese Empire. Singapore and Hong Kong were colonies of the British Empire. The Seychelles were colonised by the French Empire.

24. **Which of the following describes a feudal system?**

   A. The king did not own the land, but divided it between his barons into numerous independent states

   B. Knights farmed the land for their barons

   C. Peasants vote to elect their leaders

   D. The church belongs to the people

   E. The noble or lord has power

The answer is E.
A is incorrect, as the king remains the absolute sovereign over all the land – he merely grants land to his lords as fiefdoms. B is wrong, as it was the peasants who farmed the land which was granted to them by knights. Peasants had very little, if any, say in who governed them, as many lords came from aristocratic families. C is thus incorrect. Although church facilities and services were available to peasants, the institution belonged to the Pope in Rome, and enforced their own hierarchical system. This leaves E as the correct answer.

25. **Which individual led armies that created an empire stretching from the Danube in Europe to Egypt, and as far east as India in the 4th century BCE?**

    A. Hannibal

    B. Cyrus the Great

    C. Alexander the Great

    D. Qin Shi Huang

    E. Julius Caesar

The answer is C.
Only Alexander the Great was campaigning during the 4th century and only his empire reached this extent.

26. **In which Greek tragedy by Sophocles (497 – 406 BCE) does the protagonist inadvertently murder his own father and sleep with his mother, fulfilling a prophecy made by the oracle at Delphi?**

    A. The Bacchae

    B. Oedipus the King

    C. Medea

    D. The Iliad

    E. Prometheus Bound

The answer is B.
Sophocles' play is one of his most famous, and was interpreted by Sigmund Freud to give us the term *Oedipus complex*, which describes a youth's sexual attraction to their parent of the opposite sex.

27. **Which war took place between Athens and Sparta during the 5th century BCE, and was recorded by Thucydides – considered one of the earliest historians?**

    A. War of Pyrrhus

    B. Alexander the Great's campaign

    C. Greco-Persian War

    D. Peloponnesian War

    E. Trojan War

The answer is D.
From the choices available, the Peloponnesian War was the only one in which Greece and Sparta fought against each other. The wars lasted for almost three decades, and ended with an Athenian defeat, resulting in a short-lived oligarchy taking power in Athens.

28. **Which group of Turks ruled an enormous empire from Mesopotamia to Iran during the time of the First and Second Crusades, before being defeated by the Mongols at the Battle of Köse Dağ (1243)?**

    A. Uyghurs

    B. Ottomans

    C. Mamluks

    D. Seljuks

    E. Ayyubids

The answer is D.
The Seljuks were a Turko-Persian dynasty founded by Tughril-Beg in 1037. The Khwarazmian dynasty took over most of the Seljuk empire in 1153, but the ruling Turkish dynasty in Anatolia continued to call themselves the Seljuks of Rum, and it was these that the Mongols fought against in 1243.

29. **In November 1095 Pope Urban II gave a sermon to the French aristocracy at the Council of Clermont. The following year, what military campaign began?**

    A. The First Crusade

    B. The War of the Spanish Succession

    C. The First Balkan War

    D. The conquest of Gaul

    E. The invasion of Northern Germany

The answer is A.
In response to Seljuk advances against the capital, Emperor Alexios I Komnenos of Byzantium requested aid from the papacy. Thousands responded to Pope Urban II's speech at Clermont, slowly building up into the widespread movement of knights, churchmen, and lay people to the Holy Land.

30. **During the Age of Enlightenment, which event resulted in William of Orange invading England, overthrowing the king, and forever changing the structure of the British monarchy by inextricably linking monarchic with parliamentary power?**

    A. The Fronde (1648 - 1653)

    B. The Glorious Revolution (1688)

    C. Pontiac's Rebellion (1763 - 1766)

    D. The Jacobite risings (1688 - 1746)

    E. The Camisard Rebellion (1702 - 1715)

The answer is B.
Considered a milestone in the history of the British monarchy and parliamentary system, the Glorious Revolution led to the Declaration- and subsequent Bill of Rights in 1689, which outlined the powers held by Parliament.

31. **Who wrote *The Wealth of Nations* in 1776?**

  A. John Keynes

  B. Karl Marx

  C. Irving Fisher

  D. John Locke

  E. Adam Smith

The answer is E.
The Scottish economist Adam Smith wrote *The Wealth of Nations* during the Scottish Enlightenment. It is one of the most famous and highly-regarded early books on economics.

32. **Which of the following is an appropriate explanation of humanism, as developed during the Renaissance?**

  A. The belief that man can live an ethical and civil life on Earth by studying moral philosophy, history, rhetoric and poetry from Greek and Roman sources

  B. The belief that people as a whole should not be able to read, write, debate, or question how the people are managed

  C. The belief that humans evolved from primates, diverging about 85 million years ago

  D. The belief that we can learn nothing from Classical, pagan works of art, other than how past cultures were hedonistic

  E. The belief that we can trust certain, educated, elite individuals to properly understand the world and promote how we should live

The answer is A.
Humanists of the Renaissance in Italy believed that the essential knowledge was contained in both the Latin and Greek classical works.

33. **During the early 16th century Pope Leo X sold indulgences in order to pay for the reconstruction of St. Peter's Basilica in Rome. What are indulgences, in this case?**

   A. Beautifully illuminated copies of the Bible

   B. Holders did not have to engage in fasting during Lent

   C. Pardons for one's own sins or the sins of their family

   D. Licences to produce wine

   E. Temporarily allowed monks and nuns to engage in sexual encounters

The answer is C.
Many saw this practice as hypocritical, and caused widespread resentment which escalated with the Protestant Reformation.

34. **Influenced by both the American Revolution and Enlightenment thought, what important document advocating "natural, unalienable and sacred" human rights was signed in France in August 1789?**

   A. Rights of Man, by Thomas Paine

   B. Code of Hammurabi

   C. Summa Theologica

   D. Magna Carta

   E. Declaration of the Rights of Man and of the Citizen

The answer is E.
The Declaration of the Rights of Man and of the Citizen became France's second constitution after it was passed by the National Assembly during the French Revolution.

35. **The French National Day is July 14th, when it celebrates what event of the French Revolution that occurred in 1789?**

   A. French occupation of Nice

   B. Storming of the Bastille

   C. Napoleon's Egyptian expedition

   D. The fall of Robespierre after the period known as 'the Terror'

   E. Louis XVI beheaded

The answer is B.

the event which represents the beginning of the French Revolution. A mob stormed the prison and released its prisoners following a rumour that the king was planning on a military coup against the National Assembly.

36. **At which battle did the British destroy Napoleon Bonaparte's fleet in 1805?**

   A. Trafalgar

   B. Somme

   C. Gallipoli

   D. Culloden

   E. Waterloo

The answer is A.

At the Battle of Trafalgar, the British fleet defeated both the French and Spanish fleets off the coast of Spain. The battle lasted five hours, and although the British destroyed 19 enemy ships not a single British ship was sunk.

37. **Which of the following was the most immediate result of the February Revolution in Russia in 1917?**

    A. The formation of the USSR

    B. The Grand Duke of Muscovy took power

    C. Peter I (commonly known as 'the Great') responded by modernizing the Russian army

    D. Abdication of Tsar Nicholas II

    E. Execution of the Romanov family

The answer is D.
At the end of the revolution the tsar chose to abdicate, and sought exile to the United Kingdom. However, a year later he and his family were executed.

38. **In 1917, Vladimir Lenin started an organisation called the Cheka which was dissolved in 1922. What was the Cheka's role?**

    A. A group in charge of stimulating peaceful diplomatic relations with the Germans

    B. Build a trans-Siberian railroad to Vladivostok

    C. The governmental department in charge of collectivizing farms

    D. Early Soviet secret police

    E. Radio station primarily used to promote propaganda

The answer is D.
The Bolsheviks needed the support of a secret political police to ensure that their power was not undermined by the opposition. The original Cheka, the precursor of the KGB, was designed to investigate only crimes that worked against the revolution.

39. **The Pyramid of Cheops was built by the Pharaoh Khufu during the Old Kingdom of Egypt (3rd millennium BCE) on the Giza Plateau, and is famous around the world as one of the Seven Wonders of the Ancient World. Which of the following monumental structures is also found on the Giza Plateau?**

    A. Luxor Temple

    B. Valley of the Kings

    C. Temple of Hatshepsut

    D. Abu Simbel

    E. Great Sphinx

The answer is E.
The Great Sphynx is located on the Giza Plateau. All of the other locations are found further south, in what was known as Upper Egypt, apart from Abu Simbel which was located even further south.

40. **In what area of the world did the Second Boer War (1899 – 1910) between the United Kingdom and the Orange Free State take place?**

    A. South Africa

    B. Turkey

    C. Argentina

    D. France

    E. Belgium

The answer is A.
The Second Boer War began when Britain rejected an ultimatum that demanded that the dispute between South Africa and Britain be resolved by arbitration. It also demanded that British troops pull out of South Africa.

41. **The famous 9ᵗʰ century temple of Borobudur in Java, Indonesia, was a monument for which religion?**

    A. Islam

    B. Daoism

    C. Shinto

    D. Buddhism

    E. Christianity

The answer is D.
The monument is a Mahayana Buddhist temple, built in a form that is said to represent Buddhist cosmology. It features thousands of sculptural features, from relief panels to Buddha statues.

42. **Over 40 countries lay claim UNESCO's World Heritage status from having been involved in the material and cultural movements of the land- and maritime-based Silk Roads. Which of the following countries did the 'Silk Road' not pass through?**

    A. India

    B. Iran

    C. Morocco

    D. Jordan

    E. China

The answer is C.
The Silk Road was not one road but many roads along a route that travelled from eastern China to Europe. While the Silk Road included Asian, Middle Eastern and European countries, it never directly crossed into West Africa.

43.   What was the "Mandate of Heaven"?

    A. The name of Horatio Nelson's flagship, on which he was shot and died during the Napoleonic Wars

    B. A plot device used in ancient Greek and Roman plays to suddenly solve or conclude a seemingly unsolvable issue

    C. A document nailed to the door of All Saints' Church in Wittenberg by Martin Luther, which is believed to have started the Protestant Reformation

    D. An ancient Chinese concept of legitimacy used by the emperors to justify their rule

    E. The approval given by the Spanish crown to Christopher Columbus to make his first voyage west

The answer is D.

Tianming, or Heaven's Mandate, was a way of justifying an emperor's right to rule by demonstrating that they have the support of their ancestors. This took many forms, but the basic belief was that if society was harmonious and productive, then the emperor had the Mandate. But if society began to crumble or despair the emperor had upset the ancestors and someone else could claim to possess the Mandate.

44.   Which Chinese admiral embarked with a fleet of over three hundred ships on a series of seven exploratory voyages around Southeast Asia and East Africa the in the early 15th century?

    A. Xuanzang

    B. Hong Xiuquan

    C. Marco Polo

    D. Jiang Zemin

    E. Zheng He

The answer is E.

Zheng He set out on voyages that lasted nearly three decades at the beginning of the 15th century. His voyages left from Nanjing and travelled as far as Arabia, India and East Africa.

45. **What did the Treaty of Versailles accomplish?**

   A. Partitioned the Carolingian Empire

   B. Ended the First World War

   C. Ended the Thirty Years War

   D. Created the Vatican City as an independent state

   E. Ended the Russo-Japanese War

The answer is B.
Although it concluded the First World War, the terms of the treaty shocked most Germans through their harsh reparations, and eventually contributed enough resentment to lead to a Second World War

46. **The Russo-Japanese War (1904 – 1905) formally ended with the Treaty of Portsmouth. Which of the following is an accurate result of this war?**

   A. Russia's victory was met with sympathy and support by countries throughout the rest of East and South-East Asia, as well as confirming Western imperial superiority over non-Western powers.

   B. Japan was awarded the northern part of Sakhalin Island, though had to concede its presence in Port Arthur, Manchuria and Korea to Russia

   C. The Tsar agreed to pay indemnities to Japan, in return for keeping the important strategic location of Port Arthur and the endpoint of the Trans-Siberian Railway

   D. The Meiji Emperor's defeat forced Japan to remove their presence from Manchuria and Korea, causing them to abandon their efforts to establish imperial hegemony in East Asia and undergo a further decade of isolationism

   E. The southern half of Sakhalin Island, Southern Manchuria and Korea were ceded to the Japanese, forcing Russia to withdraw as the country faced internal revolution

The answer is E.
A and D are false, as Russia lost the war. B is incorrect, as Japan was given the *southern* half of Sakhalin Island, as well as the listed territories. C is false, as the Russians firmly insisted on not paying any indemnities and conceded Port Arthur to the Japanese. Therefore D is the only true statement.

47. **Francisco Pizarro was a Spanish conquistador that conquered which South American empire in the 16ᵗʰ century?**

    A. Incan

    B. Assyrian

    C. Teotihuacan

    D. Mayan

    E. Aztec

The answer is A.
Pizarro conquered the Inca of Peru in 1532.

48. **Which of the following is a result of the 1949 Chinese Communist Revolution?**

    A. Political power in China became unified under a stable republic led by Yuan Shikai

    B. Chiang Kai-shek proclaimed Taipei, Taiwan, as the capital of the communist People's Republic of China

    C. It sparked the "Great Leap Forward" the following year, which aimed to transform China into a socialist society

    D. Liu Shaoqi was elected as the first Premier of the People's Republic of China, and spent the following decade establishing diplomatic links with the USA.

    E. Political power in China became divided between two parties: the People's Republic of China led by Mao Zedong and the Kuomintang led by Chiang Kai-shek

The answer is E.
The Kuomintang led by Chiang Kai-shek abandoned mainland China to Mao Zedong's communist party, withdrawing to Taiwan which became officially known as the Republic of China. A is false, as Yuan Shikai was a late Qing Dynasty general and had died by this time. B is incorrect, as Taipei became the capital of the *nationalist*, not the communist, party. C is false, as the "Great Leap Forward" did not begin until 1958. D is incorrect, as it was Zhou Enlai, not Liu Shaoqi, who was the first Premier of the PRC.

49. **The Commonwealth Games is an international sporting event that is celebrated every four years by athletes from the Commonwealth of Nations. The Commonwealth of Nations is composed of which of the following?**

    A. All members of the League of Nations

    B. Countries that possess one or more UNESCO World Heritage Sites

    C. Former and current territories of the British Empire

    D. Member-countries of the Olympic Council of Asia

    E. All countries in the Arab League

The answer is C.
The Commonwealth of Nations should not be confused with the League of Nations, which was dissolved in 1946 and replaced by the United Nations. The Commonwealth of Nations is composed of territories that were freed during the decolonisation of the British Empire, but which share common values explained in the 1991 Harare Commonwealth Declaration.

50. **When referring to Canada as a realm in the Commonwealth of Nations, which of the following is an ongoing diplomatic link between Canada and the United Kingdom?**

    A. The UK is aiding Canada's attempts in becoming a member of the G20 by 2016

    B. Both countries were founding members of the League of Nations

    C. Both countries are members of the Organization of American States

    D. Over the last decade the UK has become Canada's largest source of immigration

    E. Both countries share the same monarch as head of state, Queen Elizabeth II

The answer is E.
As a commonwealth realm, Canada and the United Kingdom share the same head of state. A is false, as Canada is already a member of the G20. B is incorrect, as the League of Nations was dissolved in 1946 and does not establish any ongoing political ties. C is false, as the United Kingdom is not a member of the Organization of American States. D is incorrect, as over the last decade China has become Canada's largest source of immigration.

51. **Debates between Germany and Greece over how to overcome the Greek debt crisis have intensified since 2009, and have worsened since Greece failed to make their International Monetary fund (IMF) repayment in June 2015. One contentious solution pursued by the recent Greek Prime Minister Alexis Tsipras is a €278.7bn payment from Germany, for which of the following reasons?**

   A. To boost Greece's tourism sector, which has been overtaken by Germany's

   B. German taxpayers are amongst the worst in Europe for outstanding tax debts, and are thus hypocrites

   C. Germany has a lower population than Greece, but is much richer and can thus afford to spare the funding

   D. It will let Germany off from funding other potentially indebted governments in the future

   E. Germany owes war reparations as compensation for Nazi activities in Greece during World War II

The answer is E.
A is false, as Greece's tourism sector amounts to 24% of the country's exports, compared to Germany's 3%. B is incorrect, as German taxpayers are amongst the most diligent in Europe, with only 2.3% of tax receipts remaining uncollected – compared to Greece's 89.5%. Germany has a much higher population than Greece, making C false. D is false, as the German provision of a bailout fund for Greece would not guarantee that similar situations will not emerge in the future. This leaves A as the correct answer – though it remains a fiercely debated issue.

52. **When you plead the Fifth Amendment, what are you doing?**

   A. Defending your right to vote as an individual aged over 18

   B. Defending your right not to be enslaved

   C. Defending your right to bear arms

   D. Refuse to answer a question to prevent self-incrimination

   E. Refusing to allow an unreasonable search or seizure of property

The answer is D.
The Fifth Amendment provides the right to due process and allows the accused to prevent self-incrimination by remaining silent.

53. **Why is the constitution known as a "living document"?**

    A. It cannot be amended any more

    B. It was written on vellum (animal hide), rather than paper

    C. It can dynamically change and be edited depending on the current social context

    D. It continues to reflect the values of its initial 39 signatories

    E. It applies to all citizens of the United States

The answer is C.
The Constitution can change, and has demonstrated this numerous times throughout US history. Amendments have been made regarding the right to vote, the right to bear arms, the abolishment of slavery, and more.

54. **What does "naturalization" mean?**

    A. For a non-citizen to become a recognized citizen of a state

    B. The conquering and subsequent transformation of a nation-state by one of a different political structure, e.g. communism to democracy

    C. The process by which an urban zone becomes redefined as a rural zone

    D. To advocate and practice social nudity

    E. An educational campaign that promotes heterosexuality

The answer is A.
When a foreign citizen or national lives legally in the United States for a set period of time, they become eligible to apply for citizenship through the naturalization process. After they meet the requirements upheld by Congress, applicants must complete application, submit biometric information and undergo an interview. If approved, they become a citizen by means of naturalization.

55. **What does 'gerrymandering' refer to?**

    A. Illegally tapping communication networks, such as mobile telephones or internet connections, with the intention of blackmailing the victim

    B. It is another word for door-to-door canvassing during a political campaign

    C. Manipulating electoral district boundaries in order to achieve an advantageous result for one party

    D. The annual burning of an effigy in the form on a particularly despised politician, as a form of protest

    E. Bribing or otherwise incentivising a group of people to vote for a certain official

The answer is C.
It is generally considered an illegal practice, whereby electoral districts are redrawn to influence which group will end up becoming a majority in that constituency.

56. **Which of the following is an example of a welfare state?**

    A. Egypt

    B. Brazil

    C. The United Kingdom

    D. Russia

    E. India

The answer is C.
The United Kingdom operates a series of systems in which tax-funded programs protect the well-being of British citizens and nationals. For example, the country offers a free comprehensive healthcare service for all citizens and residents called the National Health Service (NHS).

57. What are "checks and balances", as established by the constitution?

    A. Ensuring no single branch of government has an unfair advantage or becomes too independent or powerful, by giving other branches the ability to limit the other's actions.

    B. Maintains that all people should be treated equally, regardless of race, colour, gender, physical or mental ability, or religion

    C. Gives members of the government freedom to independently implement their policies by providing funding, for which they must apply with a proposal

    D. Guarantees a regular supply of money to the country, by making it illegal to destroy cash or print your own currency

    E. Gives US citizens the right to manage their own banking affairs through web-banking platforms, though not all banks provide this

The answer is A.
They are both enabling and preventative, in that branches of government don't gain or lose power. It is split into three branches: legislative, executive and judicial, each with their own specific role.

58. Which of the following most accurately describes a socialist government?

    A. A government ruled by those who seek to enforce the will of God

    B. Active and controlling role in the economy with many government institutions

    C. Government is almost absent, with the individual freedom of the people emphasised, allowing them to make their own economic decisions

    D. A prime minister is head of state, in which they can influence the economy for only as long as they remain elected

    E. Small groups of leaders elected for their intelligence and wealth, who play a minimal role in society

The answer is B.
Socialist governments control the industries and programs that operate in the state. Instead of allowing private citizens to own or manipulate manufacturing, processing, mining or other industries, the government owns them on behalf of the citizens. Socialism true to this definition has never existed on a large scale in the modern world.

59. **What is "Common Law", when referring to the United States and England?**

    A. Regulations that restrict a government's ability to make drastic changes to the political system

    B. Laws made by collective legislature, resulting in the creation of a formal written statute

    C. The resolution of disputes between these two countries at a neutral international court

    D. System of courts that applies the law to the "common" people

    E. Judicial laws that derive their legitimacy from norms and customs developed gradually over time

The answer is E.
A lot of American law is based on the English legal system in use during the colonial era. The customs and traditions that were adopted into common law were developed over centuries in England, and maintained by itinerant judges who would roam the country to settle disputes.

60. **Which of the following is an accurate description of "Manifest Destiny", as promoted in the USA?**

    A. The belief that sovereignty is granted by the people, in exchange for protection afforded to them by the government

    B. The right of the American president to be re-elected, so as to give them an opportunity to complete their policies

    C. The belief that Americans should not be bound by British law

    D. The belief that heaven had granted US presidents the right to rule based on their moral authority

    E. The right of the American government to stretch their power over the entire continent, from coast to coast

The answer is E.
Manifest destiny was a popular form of thinking in the 19th century. The attitude inspired Americans to move westward to settle land on the West Coast. The idea supported the belief that not only did the United States have the means to stretch the country from the Atlantic to the Pacific but that it was destined to stretch across the continent.

61. What did the 1789 Judiciary Act achieve?

    A. Provided federal land grants to adults

    B. Established the federal court system

    C. Introduced the "separate but equal" doctrine

    D. Allowed citizenship in the United States by birth or naturalization

    E. Enabled the direct election of senators

The answer is B.
A federal court system was established, with thirteen district courts, three circuit courts, and the Supreme Court. These federal courts had the ability to appeal, and even reverse, state decisions

62. What was the major result of the 1965 Voting Rights Act?

    A. Prevented racial discrimination in voting

    B. Gave Native Americans the right to vote

    C. Gave overseas citizens the right to vote

    D. Gave women the right to vote

    E. Abolished property requirements to vote for all men

The answer is A.
The United States government and local governments used discriminatory practices to prevent people of colour from voting in elections. At the height of the Civil Rights Movement in 1965, President Johnson passed the Voting Rights Act. The act worked to guarantee the voting rights to all American-born and naturalized citizens.

63. **Which of the following describes "suffrage"?**

    A. The right to citizenship

    B. The right to education

    C. The right to vote

    D. The right to be free from suffering

    E. The right to free speech

The answer is C.
Suffrage means the right to vote.

64. **Medieval maps of the world are known by what name? They often serve as minor encyclopaedias, with navigational accuracy sacrificed for illustrative classical imagery.**

    A. Archaeomaps

    B. Kunyu Quantu

    C. Dymaxion maps

    D. Mappa Mundi

    E. Choropleth maps

The answer is D.
The Mappa Mundi was not designed to help users navigate geography; instead it relied on pictures rather than words to describe the world. This was because many people during the medieval period were illiterate. This meant that they were not a map in the modern sense, as much as a reflection of the zoology, theology and anthropology of a foreign land.

65. **'Mercator' is an example of what type of map projection? It provides greater accuracy around the equator, decreasing in accuracy the further away from this central line.**

    A. Polyhedral

    B. Cylindrical

    C. Azimuthal

    D. Conic

    E. None of the above

The answer is B.
An advantage of the cylindrical projection is that it can depict the whole earth in an easily understandable manner, though it does create heavy distortions in terms of direction, distance and scale anywhere beyond 15° from the equator.

66. **The concentric zone model, developed by Ernest Burgess in 1925, is most commonly used to examine what?**

    A. Urbanization

    B. Precipitation

    C. Place names

    D. Traffic flow

    E. Death rates

The answer is A.
The concentric zone model divides cities into concentric circles. These circles expand from the heart of the city into the suburbs. The model presumes an inherent relationship between household income and the geographical distance from the Central Business District of the city.

67. **When referring to the use of Geographic Information Systems (GIS), which of the following is not true about rasters?**

    A. Naturally good at handling image data

    B. Ideal for analysis of landscape

    C. Space is divided into cells of the same size (tessellation)

    D. Data is stored in a matrix

    E. Good for studying clearly bounded entities

The answer is E.
With answer C in mind, because rasters are composed of regular shapes (usually squares) they end up creating a very pixelated image. They are thus not very suitable for depicting high levels of detail.

68. **There have been several proposals throughout history for creating a bridge over which body of water separating Russia from Alaska?**

    A. Dardanelles

    B. Bering Strait

    C. Great Belt

    D. Naruto Strait

    E. Alas Strait

The answer is B.
The Bering Strait separates the Chukotka Peninsula in Siberia and the Alaskan Seward. The Bering Strait was able to be crossed by humans through an ice bridge 20, 000 years ago. Several plans to connect the two areas have been proposed; however, the cost combined with tension between the United States and Russia has resulted in the failure of every proposal so far.

69. **The contiguous United States are composed of _____.**

   A. Alaska, Hawaii, and any overseas territories

   B. 50 U.S. states, the District of Columbia, and any overseas territories

   C. 48 U.S. states and the District of Columbia

   D. 50 U.S. states and the District of Columbia

   E. 52 U.S. states and the District of Columbia

The answer is C.
It excludes Alaska, Hawaii, and all overseas territories owned by the United States of America.

70. **Which of these was a result of divergent plate tectonics?**

   A. San Andreas Fault

   B. Andes mountain range

   C. The island of Iceland

   D. Japan

   E. The Himalaya mountain range

The answer is C.
Iceland is the product of the Eurasian tectonic plate and the North American tectonic plate. These two plates have split apart over time. The resulting gap has been filled with lava, which solidified to create new land.

71. **Swash, backwash, prevailing wind, and transportation of sand are all features of which coastal phenomenon?**

    A. Melting ice caps

    B. Blowholes

    C. Wave cut platforms

    D. Wave refraction

    E. Longshore drift

The answer is E.

Transportation of sand is not a factor of melting ice caps or the formation of sea arches, so A and D are incorrect. Groins are not a feature of the creation of blowholes, which form as sea caves are extended and burst through the cliff top. Wave cut platforms are similarly not influenced by groins or the movement of sand, but instead come about when undercut cliffs collapse into the sea. This leaves E.

72. **Afghanistan can be described as going through the second stage of the Demographic Transition Model, otherwise known as the early expanding stage. Which of these are true for this stage?**

    A. High birth rate, falling death rate, rising population

    B. Low birth rate, high death rate, falling population

    C. Low birth rate, low death rate, rising population

    D. High birth rate, low death rate, falling population

    E. High birth rate, high death rate, low and stagnant population

The answer is A.

During the early expanding stage, more and more people are living to middle age and beyond. The birth rate remains at a high level, and although life expectancy is not enormous, it is certainly better than many other places in the world. This may be due to improvements made to healthcare, water supply, sanitation or diet, but the end result is a gradual increase of the total population.

73. **What name is Southern Italy otherwise known by? The region is widely studied as part of a North-South economic divide in the country, due in part to widespread corruption and violence by the mafia.**

    A. Piedmont

    B. Isole

    C. Centro

    D. Mezzogiorno

    E. Settentrione

The answer is D.
The Mezzogiorno is often studied as a periphery region. It is composed of 40% of the total Italian land area, and 35% of the nation's population, but contributes only 26% of the country's GDP. This is partly due to its rocky, mountainous landscape which prevents industrialization, though thin soils mean even agriculture is not very prolific. The area is subject to earthquakes, as well as the organized crime mentioned above.

74. **A study is made that estimates changes to network traffic following the widespread adoption of fibre-optic cables. This was in response to local demand for faster internet. What type of spatial analysis is the study likely to use when examining issues of accessibility and connectivity?**

    A. Spatial interpolation

    B. Complete spatial randomness

    C. Spatial epidemiology

    D. Spatial interaction

    E. Spatial regression

The answer is D.
Spatial interaction investigates the movement of information or people from one place to another, and in this case would examine how the desirability of the neighbourhood has changed through new opportunities for communication.

75. **In which country is the caste system prevalent?**

    A. Russia

    B. Mexico

    C. Egypt

    D. China

    E. India

The answer is E.
In India, a complex system of social hierarchy exists. It is heavily invested with Hindu beliefs, and effects many aspects of life, from the food that an individual can eat to the jobs that they can work. There are five levels to the caste hierarchy, with the "Untouchables" at the bottom and the Brahmins (priests) at the top.

76. **Which terrestrial biome exhibits these characteristics: permanently frozen soil, low precipitation, and low temperature? Example flora includes shrubs, lichens and mosses. Example fauna includes hares, wolves, and an absence of reptiles.**

    A. Mangrove

    B. Temperate coniferous forests

    C. Tundra

    D. Semiarid savanna

    E. Xeric shrubland

The answer is C.
None of the other options feature permanently frozen soil, or that particular combination of flora, fauna, low precipitation and low temperature.

77. **The current capital city of Turkey has been known by many names since its founding in the 7th century BCE. Which of the following has not been a name of the city?**

    A. Byzantium

    B. Constantinople

    C. Istanbul

    D. Stamboul

    E. Alexandria

The answer is E.
Alexandria was founded in Egypt by Alexander the Great in the 4th century BCE as a link between Greece and the Nile Delta.

78. **Which of the following would not normally cause a supply shock?**

    A. Discovery that a certain brand of aspirin causes cancer

    B. Foot and mouth disease hitting a herd of cattle

    C. Adoption of robots providing increased productivity in a car factory

    D. Hurricane Katrina sweeping over an industrial estate

    E. Discovery of a cheaper substitute for gasoline

The answer is A.
This case would cause a demand shock, as suddenly fewer people want to purchase a product that will cause them harm, resulting in a lot of unwanted, unsellable stock.

79. **What does PED stand for, in the economic sense of a commodity's ability to adapt its supply or cost based on changing circumstances?**

    A. Penny Extension Drive

    B. Price Elasticity of Demand

    C. Performance Enhancing Demand

    D. Pressured Economics Directive

    E. Personal Emergency Demand

The answer is B.
A commodity's PED can be influenced by a number of factors, based on the nature of the commodity, but can include the availability of substitute products and the variety (or lack) of uses of the product.

80. **A market is in equilibrium when:**

    A. Quantity of goods supplied is in excess of the quantity demanded

    B. Quantity of goods supplied is below the quantity demanded

    C. Buyers spend all of their money

    D. Excess demand is zero

    E. Price ceilings stop restricting free market prices

The answer is D.
A market is in equilibrium when all that is produced is sold, and nothing extra is produced or needed.

81. **Which of the following is an argument that supports the idea that university students should have to pay for their own fees, rather than the taxpayer?**

    A. The top universities are not under too much pressure, and could comfortably accept on many new students

    B. It encourages the proliferation of less conventional university courses, such as 'Surf Science and Technology'

    C. It will scare off international students, meaning that universities can accept more local students

    D. The state has more than enough money to spare, and should offer subsidies for education

    E. They are deriving private benefit from the experience, and will be the sole ones to gain from the education

The answer is E.
Many arguments against third-level education subsidization maintain that individuals who invest in the time, and expense, of attending universities are the only ones that will reap the rewards after graduation.

82. **Which of the following is not a member of the OPEC (Organization of the Petroleum Exporting Countries)?**

    A. Iran

    B. Iraq

    C. Afghanistan

    D. Saudi Arabia

    E. Venezuela

The answer is C.
Afghanistan has never been a member of the OPEC.

83. **The German government suddenly decides to impose a minimum price for Sauerkraut that is below the existing market price. The existing market price was originally higher than the equilibrium price, but what effect will this change have?**

    A. Increases supply, as manufacturers are making more of a profit

    B. Decreases supply, as manufacturers are operating on a loss

    C. Causes demand to decrease

    D. Customers now have to pay higher prices for the goods

    E. It has no effect

The answer is B.
After bringing the minimum price down to below the equilibrium price, manufacturers will find that there will be an increase in demand for the commodities, but no profits made.

84. **The USA acquires most of its oil from _____**

    A. The USA

    B. Mexico

    C. The United Arab Emirates

    D. Israel

    E. Iraq

The answer is A.
The USA acquires around 38% of its oil from the U.S. The next biggest source is Canada, which provides around 15%.

85. **What is a laissez-faire economic system?**

    A. One in which government has a total, authoritarian control over its people

    B. One in which government provides a lot of welfare

    C. One in which members of government are given special privileges and subsidies

    D. One in which government enforces widespread regulations and tariffs

    E. One in which government stays out of economic affairs

The answer is E.
The government opposes direct interference in economic affairs, beyond a minimum level. They facilitate a peaceful context within which economic affairs can be managed by the people as they see fit.

86. **When we raise the price of a product, the _____ states that this will lower the quantity required of the product.**

    A. Law of reflux

    B. Okun's law

    C. Law of demand

    D. Law of profit

    E. Law of quantity

The answer is C.
the law of demand, which states that the price and quantity of a product are inextricably linked, and changes in one result in changes in the other.

87. **Which of the following would not cause changes to a demand curve?**

   A. Changes in taste

   B. Changes in the price of the good itself

   C. Changes in consumer incomes

   D. Changes in the price of related goods

   E. Changes in preference

The answer is B.
In such a case there will be a movement along the demand curve, as opposed to a shift away from it.

88. **A person is late for work, and decides to drive in order to make up time. However, it appears that everybody else has thought of the same thing, and the driver finds that the roads are extremely congested. Which of the following would not be an appropriate description of this shared abuse of public roads – resulting in it being harmful for the group as a whole?**

   A. Overexploitation

   B. Zelinsky Model of Migration Transition

   C. Chain reaction

   D. Social trap

   E. Tragedy of the Commons

The answer is B.
This model examines the types of migration that occur in a location, but the first phase occurs only in areas that have not experienced urbanization.

89. **China's per capita water resources are only 28% of the global average, which is one of the lowest levels in the world. The scarcity of water in China today, especially drinking water, has had a devastating effect upon which of the following?**

    A. China's annual GDP

    B. growth in China's cities

    C. infant mortality in rural villages

    D. accelerated shrinking of lakes and drying of rivers

    E. all of the above

The answer is E.
China's water problems cause significant losses in China's annual GDP, stunt growth in China's cities, and have become a leading cause of infant mortality in rural villages. Hubei province was once the land of 1,000 lakes. Over the past century, its total lake area has shrunk to about 3,000 square kilometres from once 26,000. Only one of its 26 remaining lakes contains water considered safe for human consumption.

90. **Which psychological model describes the development of long-term interpersonal relationships, such as that between a mother and child, and in particular how humans respond when that relationship is threatened?**

    A. Maslow's hierarchy of needs

    B. Kohlberg's stages of moral development

    C. Attachment theory

    D. Triarchic theory of intelligence

    E. Theory of multiple intelligences

The answer is C.
It explores the nature of an infant's preference for their sole carer, especially when distressed. The way that a child is treated in these formative years can have a powerful effect on their personality later in life.

91. **An individual constantly exaggerates their own self-importance, clearly indicates that they want to be desired by everyone, and at the same time rarely shows empathy for others. These could indicate a _____**

   A. Schizotypal personality disorder

   B. Avoidant personality disorder

   C. Borderline personality disorder

   D. Paranoid personality disorder

   E. Narcissistic personality disorder

The answer is E.
as the others don't display the same lack of empathy and self-aggrandisement. A indicates discomfort towards social interactions. B indicates a heightened awareness of one's own shortfalls, and a particular sensitivity to negative comments. C indicates impulsive and harmful patterns of instability in a range of situations. D indicates a pervasive feeling of wariness towards others.

92. **Which of the following does the brain produce in its normal state when an individual is awake during the day?**

   A. Beta waves

   B. Delta waves

   C. Gamma waves

   D. Zeta waves

   E. Theta waves

The answer is A.
The other waves are produced when the brain is experiencing moments of calm or moments of heightened awareness and activity.

93. _____ is best known for focusing on the dynamics between the id, ego and superego with their psychoanalytical approach?

    A. Jean Piaget

    B. Sigmund Freud

    C. Carl Rogers

    D. Ivan Pavlov

    E. Kurt Lewin

The answer is B.
Freud's psychoanalytic theory claimed that there is a constant conflict between these driving forces in the mind.

94. **Which of the following is an example of impulsive-aggressive behaviour?**

    A. Two siblings get into an argument over whose turn it is to play on the video game console, and they resolve the situation by talking it out and reaching a compromise

    B. A school group bully a member of the class by gossiping behind their back, and always pretends to be nice whenever the individual is in their presence

    C. A member of Jane's family always rolls their eyes whenever she says something silly

    D. An individual is very insulted by a statement they overhear, but decide to ignore it and move on

    E. A car driver has to brake suddenly when a cyclist cuts in front. The driver of the car sounds their horn, shouts angrily, and speeds up so as to intimidate the cyclist.

The answer is E.
as the behaviour is reactive and hostile. A and D are passive, B is instrumental-aggressive, C is passive-aggressive.

95. **Who created a theory of cognitive development that explores the influence childhood has on the development of a person's intelligence?**

   A. Ivan Pavlov

   B. Albert Bandura

   C. Jean Piaget

   D. Sigmund Freud

   E. F. Skinner

The answer is C.
This constructivist and developmental theorist explored the skills people use to think and understand (*schema*), and how this construction of knowledge passes through various stages of development over an individual's life.

96. **What is a control group?**

   A. A group that creates the research plan, and ensures that it stays on track

   B. A group of shareholders that funds research

   C. A group that receives no treatment during an experiment

   D. A group that is studied, but the results of which are ignored in the final synthesis

   E. A group that is complete control over what takes place during an experiment

The answer is C.
The results of the test subjects that did receive treatment are then compared with the control group to evaluate the treatment's effectiveness.

97. **A schoolchild learns that when they receive good grades in class they will be rewarded by their parents with a trip to the cinema, but if they receive poor grades the trip to the cinema is withdrawn. This is an example of:**

A. Innateness theory

B. Phylogeny

C. Classical conditioning

D. Operant conditioning

E. Ethology

The answer is D.
It is the association of consequences with certain behaviours, either through positive/negative reinforcement or positive/negative punishment.

98. **An individual is convinced that a slight headache they are experiencing means that they possess a brain tumour. They are not faking the symptoms, but what somatoform disorder may they be experiencing?**

A. Hypochondria

B. Kleptomania

C. Dyspareunia

D. Bulimia nervosa

E. Erotomania

The answer is A.
It is an anxiety about one's own health that can manifest itself into actual symptoms.

99. **We are able to visualize the world in three dimensions because of which ability?**

A. Nociception

B. Peripheral vision

C. Chronoception

D. Vestibular sense

E. Depth perception

The answer is E.
A is the sense of experiencing pain. B and D are the sense of balance, movement and acceleration. C is the sense of time passing. E is an attribute of the sense of sight, though it is combined with the cognitive interpretation by the brain.

100. **Which theory maintains that people's actions are motivated by their biological impulses?**

A. Drive reduction theory

B. Disposition deterioration theory

C. Instinct decline theory

D. Impulse decrease theory

E. Motivation collapse theory

The answer is A.
The theory was pioneered by Clark Hull in 1943, and was one of the earliest to examine the role of motivations in learning and behaviour.

101. What is meant by describing someone as being conscientious?

    A. They have a tendency to promote a certain point of view above all others

    B. They have a tendency to be self-disciplined and organized

    C. They have a tendency to exaggerate their own merits or importance

    D. They have a tendency to be extremely self-aware, through regular meditation

    E. They have a tendency to be lazy and unreliable

The answer is B.
A conscientious person is often systematic, punctual, and achievement-oriented.

102. Which of the following is an example of cultural lag?

A. The technological advancement of smartphones is being readily accepted by global society, resulting in features such as touchscreens, cameras, and access to social networking being made available to a growing number of the world's population.

B. Although their status has changed in recent decades, the rights of women in Saudi Arabia are denounced by some other nations as being extremely limited, although they are considered normal and acceptable by the conservative majority within that nation.

C. A European student is attending an exchange program at a school in Beijing, and feels extremely confused, nervous and disoriented for the first few weeks of living there. This is because they react to elements of Chinese culture differently, such as unusual food, the unfamiliar language and public spitting.

D. Many members of 19th century European imperial powers, such as the British Empire and Dutch Empire, which occupied lands in Asia, Africa and the Americas, believed that the indigenous cultures were largely primitive and would benefit from their colonial presence.

E. The fertilisation of a mother's egg occurs in a laboratory environment, using the donated sperm of an unknown male. This is not fully accepted by most of society, and protests occur due to long-established ideas of parenthood, as well as ongoing debates over potential social, psychological, and legal harm that this procedure might cause.

The answer is E.
A is an example of technological acceptance, and the statement does not mention any non-material, cultural issues caused by the global use of smartphones. B is an example of cultural relativism – the belief that cultures are relative to individuals depending on their own individual context, and that ideas of "just" and "unjust" are culturally created. C is an example of culture shock, a culturally created reaction to experiencing other, different cultures. D is an example of ethnocentrism, the belief that one culture is superior to another. This leaves E as the correct answer, as it describes a situation where changes in the technological/material world are not matched by relative changes in social norms.

103. Which of the following would not make an appropriate study using a conflict-theory perspective?

A. How youth crime's relation to mainstream values being imposed on them

B. How a nation went through stages of feudalism, capitalism and socialism throughout their history

C. How social cohesion is enforced by institutions in a society

D. The factors leading to a divide between those who are most wealthy in society and those who primarily engage in labour

E. How the main economic "classes" of the nation/world create society by clashing

The answer is C.

which would be an appropriate study for a functionalist perspective.

104. In 1991, Clark McPhail's study of collective behaviour *The Myth of the Madding Crowd* identified a number of types of convergent and collective behaviour – known as his 'assembling perspective'. Which of the following is an example of collective locomotion?

A. The audience at a conference all facing the speaker

B. Everybody screams when a roller coaster begins to plunge

C. A marching band carrying their array of instruments

D. A congregation speaking *The Lord's Prayer* in church

E. Jumping for joy when your favourite sports team scores a point

The answer is E.

A is an example of convergent orientation. B is an example of collective vocalization. C is an example of collective manipulation. D is an example of collective verbalization. This leaves E as the correct answer.

105. Which of the following is a latent function of education?

A. Taught the duties of a patriotism and citizenship

B. Identify what your position in society may be after school, based on your talents

C. Realize the importance of punctuality and self-discipline

D. Started dating your classmate, who became your life-long partner

E. Taught the value of discipline by your teacher

The answer is D.
The other options are manifest functions of education– the open or intended goals within the educational system. Latent functions, by contrast, are those that were unintended, surprising, or unconsciously practiced.

106. Sociologists have noticed that in many modern nations gerontocracy has been reduced, changing the social standing of certain groups of people in terms of wealth, prestige, and job opportunities. In a gerontocratic society, who would have the most power and influence?

A. Children of the previous rulers

B. The oldest members of society

C. Younger males

D. Women who have had at least one child

E. Nobody has more power – it is shared amongst all members of the adult population

The answer is B.
The other options are manifest functions of education– the open or intended goals within the educational system. Latent functions, by contrast, are those that were unintended, surprising, or unconsciously practiced.

107. **Mothers Against Drunk Driving (MADD) is a national group attempting to change one specific thing about the social structure: to stop drunk driving. What type of social movement is this?**

    A. Resistance movement

    B. Religious movement

    C. Revolutionary movement

    D. Alternative movement

    E. Reform movement

The answer is E.
Unlike an alternative social movement and redemptive social movement, the reform movement operates on a group-or societal level. The amount of change advocated differentiates a radical or revolutionary movement, which wants to change many things in society. The secular reasoning behind MADD's proposals means B is wrong. This leaves E– a movement that is advocated by a large group or society that wants to change one specific thing.

108. **This sociologist's book, *The Elementary Forms of the Religious Life* (1912), studied the role of religion in social life by looking at totemism in Aboriginal Australian communities. Who are they?**

    A. Émile Durkheim

    B. Michel Foucault

    C. Erving Goffman

    D. Daniel Bell

    E. Charles Wright Mills

The answer is A.
This seminal text looked at how religion develops out of group dynamics. Durkheim argued that performing rituals creates a sense of "awe", which creates and protects moral norms in that society.

109. What social movement started in the 1960s, continued for two decades, and resulted in the formation of the National Organization for Women?

    A. Second Wave Feminism

    B. Anti-consumerism

    C. Arab Spring

    D. Women's Suffrage Movement

    E. Occupy Wall Street

The answer is A.
As opposed to First Wave Feminism, which focused on women's suffrage and property rights, the Second Wave advocated women's rights in the workplace, equal pay, reproductive rights, reinterpreting the role of women in the home, and sexual freedoms.

110. Which of the following studies would a social epidemiologist be least likely to study?

    A. Study how people from different countries around the world react to flu germs

    B. Examining health disparities based on gender within a school

    C. Observe how changes in religious beliefs impact the breakdown of the traditional authority of the church

    D. Critically evaluate a popular paper that claims to provide a homeopathic cure for diabetes, by investigating demographics that believe it

    E. How the communal nature of Thanksgiving dinners impact the risk of obesity in a group

The answer is C.
Social ideology examines health-related factors of society in particular.

111. **A student does not get the required test scores to move on to the next grade; however their teacher decides to move them up anyway in order for them in their intended social group. This is an example of _____.**

    A. Dropping out

    B. Merit promotion

    C. Summer school

    D. Grade retention

    E. Social promotion

The answer is E.
Dropping out involves the student leaving the class entirely, not progressing to the next level or staying in the same grade. Merit promotion allows students to move up a grade as soon as they have finished course material and demonstrated their competency, allowing them to graduate early if they have the ability. Summer schools are usually private, extra-curricular lessons. Grade retention is a system whereby students must repeat grades until they achieve the knowledge and skills required to progress. This leaves E as the correct answer.

112. **In August 1942 the Bracero Program was initiated, resulting in the widespread immigration of which "group"?**

    A. Irish

    B. Chinese

    C. Polish

    D. Mexicans

    E. Brazilians

The answer is D.
During the Second World War many Americans had left their agricultural jobs in search of better-paid employment. This left an employment gap that was filled by Mexican labourers, who were allowed to temporarily work in American farms.

113. **Which of the following is not the dominant religion in the country?**

    A. India – Hinduism

    B. Israel – Judaism

    C. Argentina – Catholicism

    D. Iran – Buddhism

    E. Saudi Arabia – Islam

The answer is D.
The dominant religion in Iran is Shia Islam.

114. **What is the reasoning behind the 'law of superposition', which is the basis of much archaeological and geological investigation?**

    A. Anything discovered automatically belongs to the country in which the investigation took place

    B. The age of material remains is indicated by their stratigraphic position, with the bottom layers being the oldest and upper layers being the youngest.

    C. It is a statement indicating the research project's strategy and methods, allowing the researchers to keep focused on specific goals

    D. 'Experts', usually academically trained, are no longer the only ones that may engage in such investigation – increasingly the public are involved

    E. Surveying provides limited information, so it is only through excavation that they can fully understand a site

The answer is B.
The law of superposition is the foundation of understanding stratigraphy – the relationships between layers of material remains. For example, in archaeology it is used in the creation of Harris Matrices when describing a site's phases of activity.

115. **Bronislaw Malinowski was an anthropologist best known for promoting which theoretical approach to social anthropology that emphasises how cultures exists to meet the cultural and psychological needs of individuals?**

   A. Functionalism

   B. Postmodernism

   C. Marxism

   D. Darwinism

   E. Cartesian dualism

The answer is A.
Malinowski advocated participant observation, and by getting a feeling of a culture's motivations developed the school of anthropological functionalism which advocated the idea that customs and institutions in a society are integrated with one another in serving human's biological needs.

116. **A survey of an historic landscape is made by a research team. The team is split into smaller groups, who cover a very large area in a short period of time. They use representative sampling strategies, and ensure that nothing on the landscape is touched or disturbed – only recorded. This is an example of:**

   A. An intensive, non-intrusive survey

   B. An extensive, intrusive survey

   C. An extensive, non-intrusive survey

   D. An intensive, intrusive survey

   E. None of the above

The answer is C.
The survey methodology covers a large (extensive) area. As the survey team do not disturb the site in any way, but instead merely record information about the site, it is non-intrusive.

117. What bias exists in the ways "Asia" has been perceived as distinct from "the West"? Edward Said used this term in his seminal book of the same name to describe how our assumptions of "the East" are actually enduring creations by European scholars, writers and observers during periods of colonial domination – changing how scholars think about power, culture, history and identity formation.

A. Axiology

B. Barbarianism

C. Indology

D. Orientalism

E. Occidentalism

The answer is D.
This book describes how our ideas of the "Orient" are discourses that are cultural constructed, and reconstructed, based on a deep history of colonialism, and perpetuated to support certain political motivations.

118. _____ is a culture's ideas of the origins of the universe, and includes beliefs on how the world and living things were created, our 'place' in the universe, and how the universe 'works'. In some cultures the influences of spiritual, non-corporeal forces play a large role.

A. Syncretism

B. Osmosis

C. Levelling mechanism

D. Astrology

E. Cosmology

The answer is E.
A refers to the merging of values or practices between cultures, or most often religions. Osmosis is the indirect accumulation of socio-cultural information. C is a cultural practice that redistributes wealth or resources within a society. Astrology involves belief in divination, and 'reading' horoscopes or the stars, and though aspects of it can be considered cosmological, it does not fit into the full definition above. Cosmology accurately meets this description.

119. **Which of the following approaches believes that one has to study all aspects of a culture in order to fully understand it?**

   A. Phenomenological approach

   B. Cultural Materialistic approach

   C. Cultural relativistic approach

   D. Functionalist approach

   E. Holistic approach

The answer is E.
A phenomenological approach advocates making use of multisensory experiences. A cultural materialistic approach focuses on the similarities and differences between cultures. Cultural relativism is an approach that advocates the idea that there is no single moral truth that applies to all cultures at all times. A functionalist approach takes a quite conservative view of society as being maintained by shared norms and values. This leaves E as the correct answer.

120. **Which of the following would anthropologists be least likely to study?**

   A. the anatomical features of dinosaurs during the Jurassic Period

   B. changes in the human body and behaviour throughout time

   C. major global transformations throughout history, such as the adoption and spread of agriculture, urbanisation, and industrialisation

   D. a country's economic and political system and opportunities provided to various social groups

   E. the relationship of a religion's material culture with their theological ideologies

The answer is A.
Anthropologists study humankind in all its workings; from material culture, to social norms, to religious beliefs and historical processes. Their focus is on humans, and as humans would have never encountered dinosaurs during the Jurassic Period – thus A would not be studied by anthropologists.

XAMonline
The CLEP Specialist

Individual Sample Tests in ebook format with full explanations

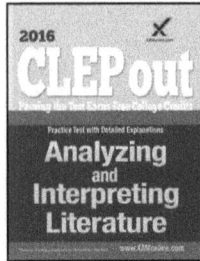

eBooks

All 33 CLEP sample tests are available as ebook downloads from retail websites such as **Amazon.com** and **Barnesandnoble.com**

American Government	9781607875130
American Literature	9781607875079
Analyzing and Interpreting Literature	9781607875086
Biology	9781607875222
Calculus	9781607875376
Chemistry	9781607875239
College Algebra	9781607875215
College Composition	9781607875109
College Composition Modular	9781607875437
College Mathematics	9781607875246
English Literature	9781607875093
Financial Accounting	9781607875383
French	9781607875123
German	9781607875369
History of the United States I	9781607875178
History of the United States II	9781607875185
Human Growth and Development	9781607875444
Humanities	9781607875147
Information Systems	9781607875390
Introduction to Educational Psychology	9781607875451
Introductory Business Law	9781607875420
Introductory Psychology	9781607875154
Introductory Sociology	9781607875352
Natural Sciences	9781607875253
Precalculus	9781607875345
Principles of Macroeconomics	9781607875406
Principles of Microeconomics	9781607875468
Principles of Marketing	9781607875475
Principles of Management	9781607875468
Social Sciences and History	9781607875161
Spanish	9781607875116
Western Civilization I	9781607875192
Western Civilization II	9781607875208

TO ORDER ➤ ✗ or amazon or BARNES&NOBLE
XAMonline.com   BOOKSELLERS

XAMonline

CLEP

Full Study Guides

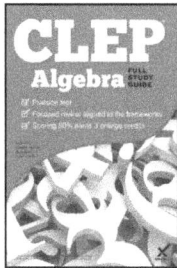

CLEP College Algebra
ISBN: 9781607875598
Price: $34.95

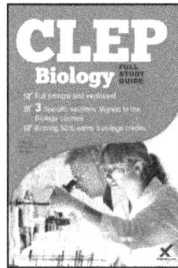

CLEP Biology
ISBN: 9781607875314
Price: $34.95

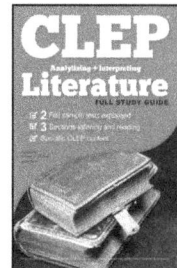

CLEP Analyzing and
Interpreting Literature
ISBN: 9781607875260
Price: $34.95

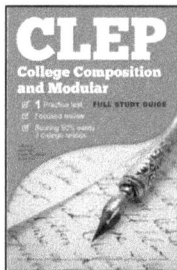

CLEP College Composition
and Modular
ISBN: 9781607875277
Price: $19.99

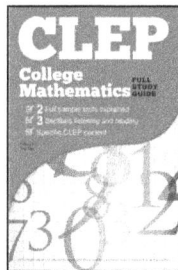

CLEP College Mathematics
ISBN: 9781607875321
Price: $34.95

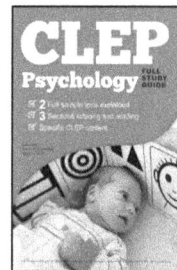

CLEP Psychology
ISBN: 9781607875291
Price: $34.95

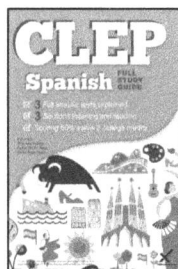

CLEP Spanish
ISBN: 9781607875284
Price: $34.95

XAMonline
CLEP Subject Series
Collection by Topic
Sample Test Approach

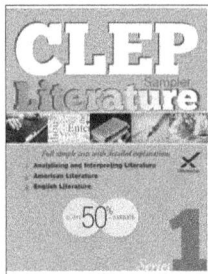

CLEP Literature
ISBN: 9781607875833
Price: $34.95

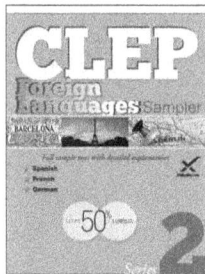

CLEP Foreign Language
ISBN: 9781607875772
Price: $34.95

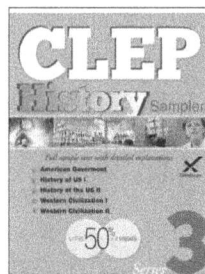

CLEP History
ISBN: 9781607875789
Price: $34.95

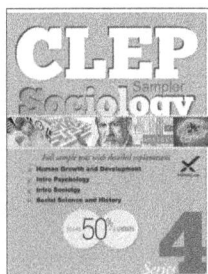

CLEP Sociology
ISBN: 9781607875796
Price: $34.95

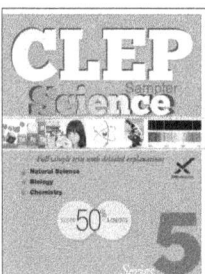

CLEP Science
ISBN: 9781607875802
Price: $34.95

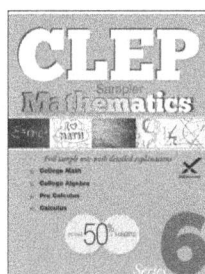

CLEP Mathematics
ISBN: 9781607875819
Price: $34.95

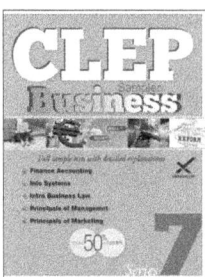

CLEP Business
ISBN: 9781607875826
Price: $34.95

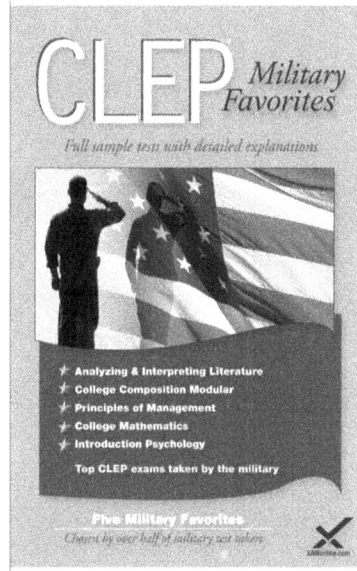

www.ingramcontent.com/pod-product-compliance
Lightning Source LLC
Chambersburg PA
CBHW080228270326
41926CB00020B/4185